THE LEGACY OF VIOLETTA ROSE

*to Anita
Enjoy the Journey,
Anjani*

THE LEGACY OF VIOLETTA ROSE

An Inter-Dimensional Journey Through the Lincoln Tunnel and Beyond

Arzani Burman

CreateSpace Publishing

CreateSpace Publishing 2008

The Legacy of Violetta Rose: An Inter-Dimensional Journey Through the Lincoln Tunnel and Beyond © 2007 by Arzani Burman

All rights reserved. No part of this book may be reproduced in any form or by any means, electronic or mechanical, including photocopying, recording, or by any information storage and retrieval system, without permission in writing from the author.

ISBN: 1438251742

Grateful acknowledgment is made to the following for permission to reprint from copyrighted material:
Coleman Barks, for his translations of Rumi, and Bright Dawn Institute, Adrienne Kubose, for the late Rev. Gyomay Kubose, for the use of his description of the Zen Koan *Bodhidharma and the Emperor Wu.*
Cover Photograph and design by Jukka-Pekka Louneva.
Author Photograph by Janet Bechtel

Drawings of the tarot cards, Six of Swords, High Priestess, and Seven of Rods © 2008 Arzani Burman

This is a work of fiction. Names, characters, places, and incidents are either the product of the author's imagination or are used fictitiously. Any resemblance to actual persons, living or dead, events, or locales is entirely coincidental.

E-mail: ArzaniBurman@yahoo.com

PREFACE

For those of you who are "preface readers," I think it may be worth your while to find out a little background to this short novel that you are about to read and I hope enjoy. I want to begin by saying that I have been a spiritual seeker since 1968 and an initiated Sufi since 1973. In addition to my Sufi studies, I have studied with a Taoist Master, a Qi Gong Master, and many teachers espousing the technique called *Advaita Vedanta,* after the great Sage/Jnani Ramana Maharshi. I have also been a student of comparative religions, and hold a masters degree in Transpersonal Psychology from JFK University in Orinda, California, and am an eighteen-year breast cancer survivor. I have been a hippie, a seeker, an art teacher, a childbirth educator, an aspiring modern dancer and a member of a '40s jazz choir, among other things—but never a writer.

Particularly because of my experiences in San Francisco in the 1970s and '80s—working at Esalen Institute and being present during a time of great influx of spiritual teachers and teachings from the East—many people have told me, "You have a book in you." But as time went by, my attachment to my past became less and less interesting. The idea of writing about what I'd learned, or experiences I'd had, seemed uninspiring and stale, and the idea of writing about them seemed like a tedious occupation at best.

Now I have already admitted to being a hippie, but I've never considered myself to be a "tree-hugger." Ironically, trying to save old growth pine trees in my neighborhood led me to writing this book.

I inadvertently had my picture published in the newspaper with my dog Layla as we protested a local developer's cutting down of trees in my neighborhood. An old friend, Anne Corssen—with whom I had lost touch—saw my picture in the paper, and over a cup of tea invited me to join her writer's group at a local bookstore. As I have already stated, I didn't consider myself to be a writer at all, but she was insistent, and so I relented.

The writer's group, called WIG (Writers Inspiration Group) was started over two years ago by Cindi Reiss and Rita Ackerman, two writers who wanted to get together with other writers to loosen up their technique and have some fun. Presently, the group consists of about a dozen people, each having some project pending—somewhere between inspiration and publication—of fiction, fantasy, journaling, history, poetry, memoirs, journalism etc. The meeting begins with a social period, followed by the introduction of very innovative prompts which each participant uses as an inspiration to write a five to seven minute piece that they can share with the group or choose to "pass." There is no criticism, and there is an overall feeling of mutual support and appreciation from the group. Since most of my previous writing involved research and outlines, this mode of working from prompts was a unique experience.

Needless to say, the WIG group taught me a very important lesson about creativity. I learned that the less I thought about what I was about to write, the better it came out. I found my characters time traveling, discovering ancient secrets and finding love in strange places. Some exercises turned into *Twilight Zone* type episodes with surprise endings. The best part was that it was always a surprise to me. I was astounded at the content that came through from my subconscious, and how well organized and humorous it could be. I started really appreciating the material and the source of the material, and still count the WIG group as my favorite activity of the week—second only to my daily private writing time.

Incidentally, I found out that this type of group is rare—and so I encourage others to try it. It's a great deal of fun and really opens up the channels of creativity. An added bonus is lots of laughter, camaraderie and chocolate.

Now that you know my secret, I just wanted to reveal that the very beginning of my book came from a prompt, and I never expected it to go more than the usual one or two pages. When it didn't end, I decided to let it go as long as it lasted, and felt sure that it would stop when it was done. Of course, this is exactly what happened, after 52,800 words. The first prompt came from a small book called *The Pocket Muse*. It simply said: "Write about someone who wins something she does not want." Another inspiration came from the Alzheimer's Association Christmas address labels which arrived in the mail that day—providing the idea for the source of the unwanted prize. On my second day of writing—which I never expected would happen—I was having coffee with a friend, explaining the use of prompts. I said, "Today I think I'll use your espresso cup as a prompt." The cup become very central to the conditions under which Alicia (Ali) meets Violetta (Vio) for the first time, and the coffee cup appears nearly every time they meet throughout the story. Later prompts were sometimes questions I had, human situations I observed, or things I saw in the newspaper. I just let them flow to see where they would go. I was delighted also to find that events and experiences from my own life found their expression in the story and became integrated with the fictional aspects, in what felt to me to be a seamless narrative.

The Legacy of Violetta Rose

I hope this bit of background will augment your enjoyment of the story of Alicia and Violetta. And now, if you'll excuse me, I'm going to pour myself a cup of coffee.

ACKNOWLEDGEMENTS

I would like to thank all my teachers, from over the past forty years, especially Wali Ali Meyer, Moineddin Jablonski, Frida Waterhouse, Harvey Grady, Joe and Guin Miller, Aiping Wang, and Nirmala. I also want to thank my husband of eighteen years, Doug Burman, who has allowed me the luxury of not having to work at a regular job so I could express my own creativity. He didn't end up in the book, but he helped make it possible and had to listen to the stories every morning as they came through.

By the way, Layla, my two-year-old Wheaten Terrier, entered the story as a dog that can appear in multiple dimensions—which often tells you something about the people who can see her when she is invisible. Including my dog in the story was suggested by my friend Jan, while I was walking Layla early one November morning.

I want to mention NaNoWriMo (National Novel Writing Month—November 1-30), which you can find on the web at www. NaNoWriMo. org. My friend Rita suggested I join and try to write a novel of 50,000 words in one month. I thought the suggestion was absurd, since every time I wrote from a prompt the story ended within a page or two. She proved me wrong, because—with the added incentive from NaNoWriMo—the story you hold in your hands (or are reading on the computer) topped the required word count, and ended at about 58,000 words in just three weeks and two days. So thanks again, Rita Ackerman and NaNoWriMo for helping me realize this seemingly impossible goal.

I want to express my appreciation to all my friends and relatives who read the manuscript in various stages of incarnation and offered feedback and encouragement to this first-time writer. And a special thank you to Suzanne Amari, Harold Michelson, Rita Ackerman and Janet Bechtel, for proofreading, and offering valuable insights, Diane Owens for copyediting and proofreading, and Jukka-Pekka Louneva for his beautiful photograph of Shanghai Tunnel and the graphic design on the front and back covers.

AUTHOR'S NOTE

I hope you enjoy this story, and perhaps find it inspiring. It is my understanding that although we are all capable of having experiences of our "True Being," "Truth," or "Unity," when we try to interpret and communicate these experiences, which are beyond words, our expression necessarily becomes influenced by our prior knowledge and beliefs. Consequently, there is no "correct" or "incorrect" interpretation of reality, since all views represent aspects of the "Truth." So, if your experience differs from Ali's, or your world view does not agree with Vio's teachings, know that your understandings are as valid as theirs, and there is no desire on my part for you to *believe* anything in this book.

ACT I

1
The Raffle

Ali took the last scoop of coffee beans from the canister, and poured them into the grinder. She pressed down the lid and was silently counting the seconds when the phone rang. *15 . . . 16 . . .* "Can't you wait a minute?" she yelled at the phone *. . . 19 . . . 20 . . .* She stopped the grinder and answered, as politely as she could manage under the circumstances. "Yes, Hello."

"Is this Miss Alicia Morgenstern?"

"Yes . . . is this a sales call, because—"

"No, it isn't a sales call. This is Mrs. Brenda Moore, of the Alzheimer's and Dementia Foundation. I'm happy to tell you that you have won the Grand Prize in our yearly raffle."

Ali recalled buying the ticket a few months back from an ambitious neighbor who rang her bell. She reluctantly gave her the ten dollar bill pretty much to stop the spiel, so she could get on with whatever it was that was so important in that moment.

"What did I win?"

A picture of the beach at Waikiki flashed before her eyes, but as she was imagining the warm sun beating down on her bare legs, the voice on the phone said: "You are the lucky winner of our grand prize, the lake house at Blue Swan Lake, New Jersey!"

"Oh . . . a lake house." Ali hoped Mrs. Moore had interpreted her monotone response as one of shock, rather than dismay.

"Yes, I know it will take a moment to sink in. We'd like you to come by on Sunday for the awards luncheon. I see by your address that you're just a few blocks away. We'll be holding it at 90th street and Lexington Avenue at our center. The luncheon will begin at noon. Will we see you there?"

"Sunday . . . an awards ceremony . . . sure, I'll be there." Ali was wondering why it was considered an "award." *I haven't accomplished anything,* she thought. *It isn't like I've won a Pulitzer Prize. I'm just "lucky," if that's what you call someone who just won something she doesn't want!*

After Ali and Mrs. Moore had said their goodbyes, Ali spooned the grounds into her coffee maker and poured in the water, as she considered the ramifications of the phone call. Up until two minutes ago, she had just about had everything in her life under control. She was a newly retired psychologist, living quite comfortably on savings, social security and the life insurance from her parents, who had died in an automobile accident when she was in graduate school.

Why has this happened to me? And why now, when I'm just about to experience my freedom for the first time in my life? I've pared down my possessions, I have free time to meditate and read and enjoy having no responsibilities. So what am I going to do with a house? And a house in New Jersey, no less.

She wasn't really expecting an answer, but from somewhere in the back of her mind she heard, *You'll see.* She ignored the voice this time—writing it off to her odd sense of humor—and poured the coffee into her cup.

Mrs. Moore looked much as Ali had imagined her on the telephone—neat white blouse, tweed skirt, black stockings, blonde hair pulled back in a French twist. She announced Alicia's name as the lucky winner of the raffle. Ali made her way to the podium where Mrs. Moore waited, dangling the keys in front of her like the golden ring on a carousel. Ali grabbed at them awkwardly, and when she finally captured them, she forced a smile and turned to the audience to deliver a short, extemporaneous speech. She thanked the Alzheimer's and Dementia Foundation for their excellent work and remarked that although her parents had died young—in an accident—she expected to live a long life and hoped that a cure for

Alzheimer's disease would be found in her lifetime. Not very inspired, she thought, but at least it was honest.

As she gazed out at the members of the Foundation, seated around their tables applauding her good fortune, she imagined their collective response to be something like: *"Why did she win it, and not me? I bought twenty tickets. I bet she only bought one."* To them, a lake house in New Jersey symbolized the key to happiness. But Ali was certain that nothing in this material world was the source of happiness: not houses, or cars, or money, or love. She just wasn't sure what was.

Ali returned to her seat at the table and as the other awards were being presented, she discreetly opened the manila envelope containing the deed to the house, the keys, and background information on the property. The house was described as a lake house at 275 Heron Lane on Blue Swan Lake—a two-hour drive from New York City—built in the early 1900s, when the lake was a quiet place with less than a hundred homes scattered around it. The reason it had been raffled off was explained in a personal letter included in the packet from Osgood Rose to Mrs. Moore. It explained that his mother, Violetta Rose, passed away and left the house to him. Because he had no attachments to the house or its contents, he felt that since his mother had died of Alzheimer's disease, it would be appropriate to donate the house to the Foundation. It seemed to Ali that the donation and resulting tax deduction—

which appeared as a gesture of generosity—was more likely an act of expediency.

As soon as Ali returned home, she looked up the address on her laptop. If the satellite map was correct, the lake house wasn't even on the lake. The picture of the roof didn't offer much detail, except that the house seemed to be set at an odd angle from Heron Lane—suggesting that it probably pre-dated the existing road. It looked small and overgrown with trees, but the smaller the better, she thought. Since she was eager to see her prize, Ali decided to go as early as she could, hoping to arrive while there was still some daylight. She changed into her "uniform" of comfortable jeans and an over-sized sweatshirt, pulled her dark brown hair back in a ponytail, threw on her coat and hat, grabbed the car keys and was off on an adventure, the scope of which she could never have imagined.

Despite her efforts to arrive before dark, the sun had long since set, and the only available light came from her headlights and the nearly full moon. She wondered where the time had gone, since she couldn't remember much of the drive since entering the Lincoln Tunnel; but she assumed an over-active mind had held her attention during the New Jersey leg of the trip. She took a side-road off the street which encircled the lake and began driving slowly, in order to see the addresses in front of the wooden Victorian homes with their wrap-around porches. The colors were ambiguous in the moonlight, and she went from one house to the other trying to read the hand-painted numbers, many having faded from the ravages of past winters. She parked the car to get a better look on foot.

As she walked up to the nearest house, a man appeared out of the shadows, yelling at her in a most uncongenial way, "What are you doing here? You're trespassing!" he growled. "Come out from under them trees so as I can see your face."

She tried to give him the benefit of the doubt until she saw the rifle pointed at her chest.

Ali had often wondered how she would react in a life-threatening situation such as this one, and despite her sweaty hands and rapid heartbeat, a seemingly composed personality emerged and took control. She stepped out into the clearing, and with her strongest voice announced, "I'm looking for number 275 Heron Lane. Is this number 275?"

"What do you want with that house? Mrs. Rose's dead and buried now."

"I just won this house in a raffle. I have the deed here and the key." She lifted up her key ring for him to see. "Please put the gun down and let me show you."

"You ain't armed, are ya?"

"No, I'm not armed. Why would I be armed, for God's sake? This is my house now. I won it fair and square. Didn't anyone tell the neighbors about the raffle?" she wondered where the phrase "fair and square" came from, but immediately turned her attention back to the man with the gun.

"I'm not much for newspapers, and I don't have no phone. My people have been here by the lake more than a hundred years. I'm the only one left now, protecting my neighbors—though I don't much like 'em. Now Mrs. Rose, she was a good woman . . ."

By the way he dropped his voice, Ali knew he had feelings for Mrs. Rose. "Well, I'm sure she *was* a good woman, and I'll bet you miss her. My name is Alicia . . . Alicia Morgenstern. What's yours?"

"Folks call me Eddie."

"Well, Eddie, if you don't mind, I'd like a hand. I can't see very well in the dark, and I've got a house to check out." Ali's request for help appealed to him. He let the rifle fall to his side and took her extended hand as they walked across the uneven cobblestone path that led to the front of the house.

As they approached the steps to the porch, he released her hand saying, "Should be safe from here on in . . ."

Ali broke the awkward silence. "So, Eddie, before you go, could you please tell me something about this house?"

"Well, this is Mrs. Rose's house all right. They mostly lived in the city. Came here with the family . . . weekends, holidays, summers. Mr. Rose passed more'en ten years back. Her son left and went off on his own. Then, after a time, she got old and sick and stayed here year 'round. Didn't see her son much after that, but she had a nurse, name of Sara . . . stayed with her until the end. Saw the boy come by here after she passed. He called her a 'pack rat' and didn't want nothing to do with her 'junk,' so he just left 'most everything as it was. I figured somebody'd come by sometime to pick it up. I just keep watch on the house . . . don't want no looters at the lake."

Ali smiled and nodded, acknowledging his vigilance, and continued walking up the wooden steps to the ample porch dominated by an old-fashioned hanging swing. Eddie followed her up the steps. She gave the swing a push to see if it still worked. The rusted chain creaked, but the swing seemed sturdy. Then she walked over to the entryway. Holding the screen door open with her back, she turned the key in the lock and pushed open the door. Eddie followed her in and closed the door behind him. As she gazed inside, she realized that without the benefit of the moonlight, the house was completely dark.

"Eddie, I've got a flashlight in my purse," she said. "It's not a gun. I'm just going to take it out now, okay?"

"Yeah, sure." he said.

Ali anticipated cobwebs and a musty smell and wasn't disappointed. She brushed the webs from her hair and turned on the flashlight, and began swinging it from left to right and back again across the dark room like a detective she'd seen on TV. The narrow light revealed a Victorian living room, decorated with cabbage roses and lace antimacassars. She felt, somehow, as if she were intruding on someone else's life, and felt oddly protective of the mysterious Mrs. Rose. In this very feminine and formal room, a man, especially a man with a gun, seemed grossly inappropriate.

"If it's okay with you, Eddie, I think I'm safe here now, and I'd like to look over the place by myself. I appreciate your accompanying me here, and I'm grateful to you that you'll be watching over the house for me—but right now I want to see exactly what I've won."

This diplomatic tone worked well and without uttering another word, Eddie was halfway out the door when he hesitated, turned and said, "Mrs. Morgan, is it? I'll be right outside, just in case you need me. You don't know if there ain't somebody holed up in there."

"Thanks, that makes me feel much safer. . . and it's Morgenstern." (She thought it better not to correct the "Mrs.")

Ali shut and locked the door after him, grateful to be alone at last. She took a deep breath, regained her composure and moved slowly into the parlor. Despite the cobwebs, it looked to be a room that welcomed friends for tea, cakes and conversation. There were velvet chairs, printed wallpaper, and doilies on the arms and backs of the chairs and couch. The carpet also had a floral pattern, and although nothing matched, it seemed comforting, in a grandmotherly kind of way. She wondered if there was central heating, but her question was answered as she nearly tripped on a grate in the floor. She assumed the house was well equipped with fireplaces, and indeed she was correct. She found one in the living room, one in the dining room, and expected to find one in each of the bedrooms as well. The downstairs hearths were all decorated with ample mantles covered with cards, statuettes, photographs and small souvenirs which gave her an added appreciation for the past inhabitants.

Ali stood before a beautifully carved wooden staircase. She walked halfway up, but then halted. On this first day of exploration, she felt it would be a violation to go into a stranger's private quarters. She somehow needed to know Mrs. Rose better before she ventured further. It was as if she were awaiting an invitation, although this was very unlikely, given the circumstances.

I think this is enough for one day, Ali thought, as she held onto the banister and stepped backwards to the landing. And although she hadn't changed her mind about winning the house, she had to admit she felt strangely "at home" here on Heron Lane.

As Ali walked out into the darkness, she turned the key in the lock, jiggling the knob to make sure the house was secure.

"See you later," she yelled out into the empty night. She made a mental note that the next visit might best be made in the daylight.

2

A Cup of Espresso

Ali woke up bright and early Monday morning—maybe not so bright, not before her first cup of coffee. As she searched the cupboard for the last bag of the holy grind, she thought about how well suited she would be to the nomadic life, contingent, of course, on the availability of coffee. *Lawrence of Arabia had coffee, didn't he, or did he remain a tea drinker?* Her search for the elusive beans led her to the terrible discovery that she was totally out. Since she had made a promise to herself to get to the lake house quickly—before Eddie had a chance to notice her—she made the fateful decision to follow her intention and forego the coffee.

She grabbed her purse, some energy bars and her maps, and before shutting the door, glanced back to make sure she had everything. *Keys?* Back in the apartment she retrieved her keys from the kitchen table, closed and locked the door and took inventory again. *Okay, I've got everything now.* Secure that she was prepared, she took the elevator to the garage, retrieved her car and began the two-hour drive from Manhattan—through the Lincoln Tunnel—to the sleepy summer resort town of Blue

Swan Lake, New Jersey. Since she was traveling against rush hour traffic, she made good time and arrived safely.

She parked on the side of the house, at the end of a driveway which led to a detached garage about seventy-five feet back in an overgrown but somehow charming yard. The lake was across the road, so the backyard was private, with shrubs and trees which gave the appearance of an abandoned English garden. And although Ali was not much of a romantic, this particular garden seemed very mysterious and oddly enticing. The very thought of gardening was foreign to her and a bit unsettling; but she attributed the feeling to her lack of caffeine, and continued her inspection by following the cobblestone path around to the front of the house.

With the benefit of daylight, Ali was able to get a better look at the dark green house with delft blue trim and the stairs she had so carefully ascended to the porch the night before. Everything looked a little shabby, but certainly less spooky. The porch swing was indeed operational, although the fabric on it was frayed on the edges. Obviously no one had taken it inside for the winter. It was, nevertheless, still inviting—but not right then. As she approached the door, she saw, just above the entryway, a hand- painted wooden sign with the words "Rose Cottage" in ornate Victorian-style letters.

Ali opened the door and met with her first full view of the entryway. The cobwebs were still there, but through them she was able to see a comfortable sitting room. Since she had gone directly to the stairway the previous night, she realized there was more to see on the first floor. She moved through the parlor and dining room—passing the staircase—and then turned to the right and entered a large, inviting kitchen with tall white cabinets that went all the way up to the high ceilings, and a black-and-white tiled floor. There was a small, elaborately carved round table and two chairs with flowered seat cushions.

The room had nothing much to distinguish it from any other kitchen of that era until she noticed on the table a single white cup and saucer, espresso-sized. *Ah, Mrs. Rose enjoyed espresso too.* The cup was filled to the brim with coffee. *How odd,* she thought, *that no one has cleaned the place after the old lady died.* Little did Ali know that this would be her last thought supported by the reality she had previously embraced. Even more strange, the coffee was hot.

She wrapped her fingers around the small cup. *Maybe it's just hot in here and my mind is playing tricks. Or maybe someone is squatting here. Where is Eddie, when you need him? Maybe Mrs. Rose is not dead at all!* Ali visually searched the room for any evidence of an espresso machine. Even a drip coffee maker or a steaming pot on the stove would do, but she saw nothing. As she frantically opened one cabinet door after the other, she found no coffee makers in any of the cupboards, above or below. Barely avoiding hitting her head on an open cabinet door, she returned to the table. She sat down and pondered the situation, but her mind could offer up no explanation. Dare she take a sip to see if this was her imagination playing tricks? She brought the steaming cup up to her lips and just let the vapors reach her nose. *Yes, this is really espresso, really fresh, and really impossible.*

Okay, not to worry, she tried to assure herself. *There just must be someone here. It's time to explore the rest of the house.* "Is anyone home?" Ali called out. *Maybe there's someone in the bathroom.* She knocked on every door, even the closets. Receiving no response, she carefully opened each door and determined that the ground floor was empty. *Maybe upstairs*, she thought. Ali ran up the stairs, this time forgetting to hesitate or ask permission. There were four doors. She assumed there were three bedrooms and a bathroom. She went from one to the other, knocking, listening and then gingerly opening the doors. There was a small staircase at the end of the hall which she guessed led to the attic. She knocked on the door and turned the handle, but the door was locked. On a hunch, she ran back outside and took another look at the house. In the daylight, she saw that on the far left side of the house, a round turret room rose just above the second floor.

She ran back into the house, up the main staircase to the second floor and ascended the steps at the end of the hall. She pulled the key ring from her purse and saw the second key—which she had assumed went to the padlock on the garage door. It had the look of a skeleton key, and when she tried it, it seemed to slip in the lock. Turning it to the right and left accomplished nothing. She jiggled it impatiently until finally it engaged and the lock clicked. With a shove of her right hip, the narrow arched door opened.

As she entered the room she first noticed the beautiful curved glass Victorian windows with scarlet velvet draperies pulled to the side, revealing a beautiful view of the lake. There was a lovely old desk, shelves piled high with books, and a small settee just perfect for reading. As Ali gazed through the old glass, she saw the lake on the west and the garden on the east. On the north side she could see a neighbor's house nearby, but none on the south side. The north, she recalled, was the direction Eddie came from with his rifle, but she couldn't discern which house might be his.

Standing in this special room, she could sense the presence of Mrs. Rose and momentarily forgot the purpose of her search, which was looking for intruders. Since she was now satisfied that there was no one else in the house, how could she explain the hot coffee? Why was it placed right where she would see it? And who knew that was exactly what she needed? But she knew, somehow intuitively, that the answers would have to wait for at least another day.

3
Introducing Violetta Rose

On her third trip to the lake house, Ali went directly to the kitchen to see if the apparition was still there. Yes, the coffee was still steaming. As she lifted the cup to her lips — against her better judgment—she felt as if her arm was moving before the decision was even made. And as she poured the warm liquid into her mouth, she wondered, for a split second, about the concept of "free will." *Ah, this is surely the best cup of coffee I've had ever tasted.* She swooshed the liquid around in her mouth for a moment or two, almost not wanting to swallow, just so she could prolong the experience a bit longer.

She looked across the table from where she was sitting and saw a toaster, and a tea pot covered with a quilted tea cozy sitting on the counter. But the scene seemed out of focus, as if she were looking through the steam coming off the top of an old radiator. She rubbed her eyes and tried again—the reason for her blurred vision now becoming apparent. She was looking through the form of an elderly woman with white hair done up in a bun, wearing an apron, sitting opposite her, sipping tea.

"Mrs. Rose? Mrs. Violetta Rose?" Ali asked.

As the apparition began to speak, her body took on a more solid form—not quite normal, but more translucent than invisible.

"Yes, Alicia. I'm Violetta Rose. I was so pleased when you bought that raffle ticket for my house. I was so hoping it would fall into good hands."

So many questions came to Ali's mind that she didn't know which one to ask first: *Is she really dead? Can she read my mind? What does she want from me? How did she know I wanted coffee? Why did I drink it? Am I insane?*

"How did you know I wanted coffee?" Ali reflected that this was an interesting choice for a first question—but she was known to be blunt, and the coffee did loom large in her consciousness. Since Violetta smiled but did not immediately respond to that question, Ali decided to try another one. Even though she had what seemed like a few minutes to formulate her second question, what came from her lips was the very straightforward "Aren't you dead?"

"Yes, you might say I'm dead to your dimension, but very much here in mine, don't you think?"

Ali decided to do a sanity check. *Here I am, sitting at the kitchen table, sipping espresso with a ghost who says she's living in another dimension. How do I address a ghost anyway?* Rather than blathering on with some more inane questions, she decided to turn the floor over to Mrs. Rose.

As if Mrs. Rose had read her mind, her first response was, "Please call me Violetta, or Vio, if you'd like; and I'll call you Ali. As you now know, I am still living in my house (or your house now). I hope you will invite me to stay. I will make certain your needs are met, from my plane, but you'll probably want to have the utilities turned on from yours."

Ali wondered why she hadn't been cold on her previous visits, but then noticed there was a fire burning in the dining room hearth.

"Oh yes, my dear. I can't pay the bills in this form, and I think the gas company might find it strange if I could; but I did light some fires for you to make you comfortable. I so want you to return, you see.

"I hope the coffee was to your liking. Others in your position might think this house is haunted, but I know you can tell that I am not that kind of spirit.

"When you took that first sip of coffee, Ali, I heard you ask a very interesting question that you might not think to ask me right away. In fact, I think you said it under your breath from a cynical point of view, but I'll answer it for you anyway. You wondered if you had any choice in whether or not you'd actually drink the coffee. I will tell you now—although you may not understand it just yet—that it may appear that you had a choice, but the person you believe yourself to be didn't really have a choice at all."

"But I make choices all the time, don't I? I bought the raffle ticket." Ali argued.

"Sometimes things, indeed, will go the way you thought you chose. But often they don't—and not always to your detriment, I might add. You might like to take the invitation to search for the source of that original impulse, the one that made you lift the cup. But enough of that for now."

Ali cocked her head to the left, and looked at Violetta incredulously, but could not avert her gaze from Vio's nearly transparent blue eyes.

"Not to worry. I know it's a frightening idea, but when you experience the truth of it all, it will feel just right and perfect the way it is. I also want to set you free of any idea that you might be possessed by the spirit of a dead woman. Yes, I know that was on your mind. The being calling herself Violetta Rose—as you experience me now—doesn't have free will either. We are all under the loving supervision of something greater than ourselves which is all inclusive. The ironic thing is that separate beings will never understand what I have just said.

"So, enough with concepts. You've had enough of those in your lifetime to fill a library. It's time for experiences. Just don't be afraid, Ali. Everything is going according to plan. I knew it when you drank the coffee. That showed me that you were willing to suspend belief and step into the unknown. You don't know how I rejoiced when you took that first sip."

"You probably know I'm not the adventurous type. You made the right choice in setting the coffee before me. That was probably one of the only reasons I would take such a risk."

"You sell yourself short, my dear. You came to this house when you really didn't want it; you entered, despite the gunman who tried to stop you in your tracks; you returned and drank the 'brew,' and now you are still quite excited at the prospect that a new mystery is unfolding for you. You have a new partner in your life, a dead old woman to be exact, and you are about to embark on a journey for which you have no training or prior experience, and yet I can sense your excitement."

Violetta put down her teacup. "So I think you are the adventurous type. Perhaps it is a part of you that you are just getting to know. And yes, by the way, I don't need to eat or drink anymore, but I so love tea that I continue the ritual. It makes such a lovely way to talk together, don't you see? I think you probably enjoy my appearance as well."

"Oh yes, I find your appearance most beautiful, and the surroundings, although dusty, very inviting."

"Please excuse the house. It's been a while since I've had visitors. I'll have that cleaned up for you right away. And anything you wish, we can make it happen for you. But I honor your desire to be simple and to the point. As we move through realities, it's best not to carry a lot of baggage."

"What kind of plans do you have for me?" Ali asked.

"In all honesty, this is as new for me as it is for you. The coffee cup was actually my first trick, and appearing here to you, my second. I've only been gone for about three months—although, since I 'lost my mind' I was able to do some traveling back and forth, a kind of reconnaissance, if you will. But more about that later."

Violetta took Ali's hand in hers. It felt very soft and gentle, but reassuring at the same time. As Violetta released Ali's hand, she placed her hands over her own heart, bowed and said, "Ali, it has been a pleasure meeting you. I hope I will see you again soon—tomorrow perhaps?"

"Tomorrow, oh yes!" Ali found it difficult to take her eyes off this amazing apparition, but she didn't want to overstay her welcome, so she turned and walked toward the door.

Ali turned back one last time, but Violetta had disappeared. She did note that all the cobwebs were gone, and the place looked vacuumed and swept. On her way to the car, she saw the garden was well manicured, and flowers in colored pots lined the path to the driveway.

4
Haiti

Ali remembered driving into the Lincoln Tunnel, and then the next thing she knew, she was turning into the driveway on Heron Lane. As she pulled up to Violetta's house (it would always be Violetta's house, regardless of the name on the deed), she said a prayer of thanks to whoever had been doing the driving.

The yellow and purple flowers in colorful pots lined the pathway as she remembered from the previous day. *So yesterday wasn't a dream*, she thought. The stairway to the porch still creaked as she jogged up the steps and stopped at the front door with the "Rose Cottage" sign above. She rang the bell and then turned her key in the lock. She announced herself from the doorway, and entered. She walked across the floral patterned carpeting of the parlor and dining room into the shiny black-and-white tiled kitchen, and there was Violetta, sitting at the table with a tea pot and delicate china cup for herself, and the espresso waiting for her guest.

"So, Ali, how will we keep ourselves occupied today?" She heard Violetta respond to her thought. "Your guess is as good as mine. And yes, Ali, you are correct in assuming that your thoughts are now public domain. Let me also remind you that I see you as a perfect, imperfect human being, playing your role beautifully. I will not condemn you for your words or thoughts, and you can never disappoint me. I'll let you in on another secret. When you are dead, as I am, nothing is at stake, and so there is no fear. I will be reminding you of that from time to time.

"I think the best way to start would be for us to go up to the turret room and see what awaits us there. Is that agreeable to you, Ali?"

Ali's answer was, "Agreeable? Absolutely!" Her enthusiasm was something she couldn't hide, but then why should she even try?

Ali made her way up the two flights of stairs, and Violetta — although she didn't know how Violetta got up there—met her inside the doorway.

"This room is a portal, a doorway to other dimensions. So let's look around and see if there are any clues about where we're to go this morning."

Ali noticed an inkwell and a fountain pen on the desk, and a clean sheet of white paper. As she looked at it, the pen began to write, and the message was simple. "It's time for you to take a vacation."

As Ali read the words, the floor disappeared beneath her, and she experienced herself in free fall. She landed softly on a sandy beach. She brushed the sand from her clothes and turned to see Violetta beside her. Vio, who didn't seem to need to brush herself off, asked simply, "Have you ever been to Haiti before?"

"No, I haven't. I've been to Hawaii, but never the Caribbean," replied Ali, as she pulled off her shoes and poured out some sand.

"I believe you have, Ali, in a dream you had about thirty years ago."

"Now how would you know that? I've never told you my dreams."

"No, you haven't, but we were brought here because of you—of that I am certain. Do you remember when you were last here?"

"Okay, yes." Ali had to admit. She turned a full 360 degrees, taking in all the scenery around her. She saw a boat in the harbor, and as she turned toward the shore, she saw beautiful pastel-colored houses and a white shack with a thatched roof, just far enough from the water to avoid the tides. "Yes, it looks very familiar. As I turned, I already knew what I would see."

"Tell me about the dream, Ali."

"In the dream, I was shown my birth onto the earth plane. Haiti was a symbol of Earth—or maybe duality— because it had both the beauty and grace of the native people, the pastel colors, the palm trees and the sea, but also the ugliness of war, greed and corruption. I was offered Earth as a landing place, and I made the choice to stay. It seemed that I had sailed in on a boat, just like the one you see in the harbor now. On the boat were my parents, delivering me to a native woman in a white dress with white fabric wrapped around her head in the island style. She carried me in her arms onto the shore and took me to a little shop . . . it was exactly like that one right here on the beach. Behind the front counter stood a woman dressed in bright orange native dress. In the display case were various items, and I was instructed to choose only one. I chose the tarot cards. They looked familiar to me in the dream, but they were hand-made and outlined in black, like a coloring book. When I chose them, I was told they were a very good choice and were all I needed to *remember*. I asked why they were in black outline, and the woman answered that it would be my job, in this lifetime, to color them in. But how could you have known that, Vio? It was only a dream."

"On one level it seemed like a dream, but on the other level it was true—and that is the level I live on all the time. The place you call 'reality' to me is a dream, but from another view it is also real. I went into your dream to bring you into my reality, and here in Haiti, you see, our realities meet."

Ali paused for a moment to take in what she had just heard. She felt suddenly energized. "Okay, Vio, what are we here to do?"

"We are here for you to retrieve what you lost. Do you own a deck of tarot cards?" Vio asked.

"I have the *Rider-Waite* deck at home. I often use them to help make choices."

"Do you remember what I said before about choices?"

"But I *chose* to come here with you today, didn't I?"

"Did you? Which came first, Ali, the thought or the impulse?"

"The impulse, I guess. Everything, recently, seems to be that way. It's all very new for me."

"You believe it's new for you, but in reality it always has been that way. You only think your thoughts come first. The impulse comes and then the thought, and then the owning, and then the grief over the decision you never made in the first place. What if there were no choices, but only *what is?*"

Ali felt her body suddenly relax, and she felt very light. "There'd be a lot less stress, that's for sure—no remorse, no guilt, no comparison. Just hearing that makes me feel so much freer. But isn't it really saying I'm not free at all?"

"That's true, Ali. The part of you that longs for freedom is not free, but the part of you that is already free gets to rejoice in its true being. You'll see."

"Violetta, is there no agenda here for us today? What are we to do if we can't make choices?"

"Look straight ahead of you, Ali."

"That's the spiritual prescription? I just should look straight ahead of me all the time?"

"No, Ali. There is no prescription. I really mean look straight ahead and see if that store is the one you saw in your dream, the dream where you *chose* the tarot cards.

"Let me pose this question for you, Ali, before we go in. Did the character in the dream choose the cards, or did you, the dreamer? I don't want an answer."

"Okay, Vio. I won't give you an answer to that—as if I could. But I will answer the first question. That was the store in my dream. It was a simple white building with no door, just an opening in the front. There was only one counter, which faced the entrance; and there was a native woman, dressed in a brilliant orange dress and headpiece, standing behind the counter." They walked through the doorway, and the tarot cards were displayed, drawn in black outline, just as Ali remembered them.

"Ali, you know that the purpose of the cards is much greater than for making so-called decisions. They are archetypes which represent all aspects of human existence. That is why you chose them in the dream—so that you could learn to be human and to appreciate the gift of incarnation."

Ali sighed, and took that all in. "Of course, that's why she said, in the dream, that the deck was all I needed."

"Let's ask if we can have a reading. I'll bet the woman behind the counter can help us out."

Ali stepped forward and greeted the woman in French. "*Bonjour.*" Before she could continue, in her high school French, the woman responded in excellent English.

"Good day, and how can I help you today?"

Ali asked if there was someone who could read the cards for her. The woman came out from behind the counter, introducing herself as Simone. Ali noticed she was barefoot and dressed in her native costume of orange and gold, even more beautiful than she remembered in her dream. Simone motioned to Ali to come sit at a small table with two chairs behind a screen. She pulled out a chair for Vio also. Ali wasn't able to determine whether Simone was living on the other dimension, or if the three of them were in a dream together, but she accepted it for what it was.

When all three women were seated, Simone spread the deck across the table, face down. The backs of the cards had a beautiful iridescent pattern that sparkled in the sunlight. She instructed Ali to choose three cards. Ali took a deep breath to center herself, and delicately pulled three shimmering cards from the deck, still face down on the table. Simone nodded in approval and began her reading.

"The first card represents the *Self*, the second card, *Situation*, and the third card, *Opportunities*." Simone turned over the first card in the position of *Self*. She closed her eyes for a moment, and then looked directly into Ali's eyes. Ali braced herself for what she feared would be bad news.

"The card you chose is the *Seven of Rods*, sometimes also called *Seven of Wands*. This card is a card about success. In the card, you are shown as a warrior, vanquishing six opponents, because you have the advantage of being above them. Do you feel this describes you accurately?"

Ali's confidence grew from this short description, and she sat up straighter in her chair. "Yes, although I don't see myself as a warrior, I have recently retired from what you could call a successful counseling practice, and I've taught classes on spirituality and healing, but sometimes I have been described as being 'aloof'—and I don't believe that is a positive characterization."

"I see. This card does apply in a very obvious way, because I must tell you that this card also carries a warning. It warns of a false sense of smugness. Do you see how the warrior might feel aloof? It suggests that you don't confuse success with being invincible, because that might cause you to follow your ego rather than your guidance. Do you understand what I'm saying?"

"Oh yes. I think it's very good advice." Ali wished she could take back what she said about being aloof, but part of her remembered that there was nothing to hide.

"Ali, I must tell you that although I am issuing a strong warning to you, this is a card generally used to indicate success. The warning I am giving you is because the task you are taking on with Violetta is much more challenging than any earthly battles, and so you are a special case in that regard. Do you understand?"

"Yes, I think I do. But how hard is it? I don't even know what I'm taking on."

"I trust this will unfold.

"Now, let's move on to the second card, in the position of *Situation*. You have chosen the card I knew you would choose. I saw you as the *High Priestess* when you walked in today. Of course you are the High Priestess on the higher planes, but your work is to learn who she is on the earth plane as well. If you'll notice, she is sitting between two pillars, each labeled with a letter. They represent the positive and the negative poles."

"Oh yes, I know, the 'B' stands for *Boaz* and the 'J' stands for *Jakin*."

"I see you are a student of the tarot. What is most important here is that you understand what it is to be between the two poles and in acceptance of them. The equilateral cross she wears is a representation of how there can be a union of positive and negative, which results in Eternal Knowledge."

"Yes, I know, it's like *Yin* and *Yang*, isn't it? I know about that. I just wish everyone knew this, especially our politicians."

"Ah, Ali, I am heartened that you are aware of this concept, and my wish for you is that you will go beyond the conceptual, and experience the merging of the opposites. I believe Violetta will help you with this. It is something you can never conceive of with the mind, because the mind is built to see opposites and contrast."

"You mean like a cat can only see moving objects?"

"Something like that. Yes, very much like that. Since you chose this card, I have confidence that you will achieve this knowing very soon. Another aspect of the *High Priestess* is that she sits in a position of objectivity—but not aloofness, you see.

She is seated on the earth, not on a hill above, like your first card. She can be objective while allowing herself to experience the negative and the positive, finding the wisdom that lives within the two. And her wisdom, Ali, does not come from judgment, or opinions, or critical thinking. This will be a wonderful learning for you.

"The third card you have chosen, Ali, in the position of *Challenges and Opportunities* is the *Six of Swords*. It is about turning obstacles into stepping stones. Looking at the picture, you see the ferryman. His job is to take people to the other shore. It sometimes means leaving what is familiar for a new country, or a new way of being. For you, this could mean a changing of dimensions, from the earthly dimension to the heavenly."

"It reminds me of Herman Hesse's book *Siddhartha*. At the end of the book, Siddhartha reaches enlightenment and becomes the ferryman. It is a very powerful symbol for me." Ali added.

"Yes, and when you recognize who you truly are, you will know, intimately, what you are describing to me today. I hope this reading has helped you to recognize your task, and how Violetta will serve you. It seems very appropriate, and I hope it will assist you in reaching your goals." She put her hand on Ali's back and patted it gently. Ali felt a warmth move into her heart, alleviating the fear that had unexpectedly taken over when she saw her task laid out for her on the table.

"Thank you so much, Simone. I believe it has been a great help."

Simone looked directly into Ali's eyes and placed her right hand on Ali's left shoulder and her left hand on Ali's right shoulder. A chill went through Ali's body, and she felt she had been blessed. Then Simone nodded, turned and walked behind the counter, but this time parted a curtain and disappeared from view.

"It's amazing to me how appropriate the cards seem to be," Ali said to Vio. "I understand the Jungian concept of synchronicity, but I feel, intuitively, that there is something more universal that underlies that theory."

"Yes, I believe that is true . . ." Vio replied, "and I will leave it to you to discover the answer to that question. Is there anything else you would like to ask?"

"Yes, Vio. How did Simone know my name?"

"She knows your name because she is in your dream, Ali. She is your creation."

"Violetta, this is getting very interesting. I'm eager to see what comes next. Will we be staying here in Haiti?"

"I don't believe we will," Violetta responded, as they both found themselves being lifted into the air and back into the turret room of Rose Cottage.

"That was a long way to go for such a short time."

"How long was it really? It was instantaneous. You must learn to see what is in front of you in the light of your new understandings. No place is far away, and no time is long or short when seen from the viewpoint of heaven. *Á demain*, Ali. I'll see you tomorrow."

The drive home again seemed outside of time, for which Ali was grateful.

5

Switzerland

Ali awoke suddenly, from a nightmare. She could hardly breathe, her heart was pounding, her body stiffened and her shaking hands had formed into fists. *What's going on? I feel like I could kill someone! But who?* When the physical sensations finally subsided, she closed her eyes and tried to reconstruct the dream. A face came into her field of vision that she recognized as her first lover, a handsome Danish student named Johan. Within the first week of classes, he had stolen her heart, proposed marriage, and then, just as quickly, returned to Denmark to marry his ex-girlfriend. Ali was re-experiencing all the feelings of anger, jealousy and betrayal, as if forty years hadn't passed.

As the morning progressed, Ali returned to her morning routine, and the effects of the dream began to diminish. By the time she arrived at the lake, her focus had returned to the present, as she anticipated her visit with Violetta.

It was about ten o'clock, and Ali was on the path from the driveway to the house. As she walked up the steps to the porch, she noticed that the chains on the swing were shiny and rust free. She sat on the swing for a moment, just to ponder the changes she'd experienced and the lessons she had learned the previous day. To the right of the swing she saw a small round wicker table with a glass top. Centered on the table was a decorative saucer with her cup of espresso. She wondered where Violetta was. As she lifted the cup to her lips and took a sip, Violetta appeared beside her on the swing. Ali noted that the weight on the swing had not changed, but the beautiful old lady with the white hair pulled tightly into a bun was unquestionably there.

"How was your night? Did you sleep well? Any dreams?"

"Funny you should ask me that. I had a nightmare about a man I hadn't thought about for at least forty years. I woke up very angry and disoriented."

"Do you think the changes you have gone through in the last two days might be described as a disorienting experience?"

"Disorienting might be an understatement." Ali responded.

"Making a commitment to move between the two worlds can have some repercussions, physically and emotionally. In metaphysical terms, you are moving between the worlds of the seen and the unseen, and on the psychological level, in terms I'm sure you are familiar with, more material will be moving between the subconscious and conscious levels of your psyche. This is done in order to clear out the heavy, unincorporated material so that you can live in the present. This will also make you lighter so you are able to 'travel' more easily. Don't be surprised if things start surfacing that you thought were resolved."

"Thanks for explaining that. It helps. But knowing that, I'm still eager to find out what today holds for us."

"It's not I who has something for you today. Make no mistake about that. We are being played together. We're a team and only the 'writer' knows what there is in store. Would you like to join me in the turret room?" They met again inside the doorway, and both walked toward the desk—Ali with apprehension, Vio with confidence. On the empty pad, the pen began to write: "Find a mountain climate to your liking, and have a climb."

"Do you think it means a climate, as in weather, or in mood?" Ali asked.

"Perhaps both. How about a trip to the Swiss Alps?"

Before Ali could even turn around to ask Vio her next question, they were lifted up, this time through the roof of the house. The sensation of wet coolness was the first indication for Ali that she was sitting on snow. The original discomfort shifted immediately to one of awe when she took in the vista surrounding her. Everywhere she looked, the mountains rose in their white-capped glory, and nestled between four peaks was the most beautiful lake she'd ever seen. It was not the typical blue color of a lake that reflected the sky, but the purest turquoise, sparkling in the sunlight. She knew this was a vision she would never forget, because she felt she was not seeing it for the first time, but remembering it.

Vio sat beside her, enjoying the spectacular view, and Ali, after drinking in the scene for as long as she could without thinking, finally turned to her with the obvious question, "Well, here we are. Now what?"

"It looks like we've landed in the middle of a guided bus tour of Europe, Ali. You have joined the tour in Lucerne, and the tour guide, André, will be introducing you to the group. I will tell you about André, and then it will be up to you to do some detective work on a mother and daughter who are here on vacation. I'll point them out to you when I see them, but you will need to fill in the details."

"How am I supposed to do that?"

"Come on, Ali. You know how to get peoples' stories. You're a counselor, aren't you?"

"But they're not willingly coming to me as clients, are they?"

"No, but you are familiar, I'm sure, with the 'airplane syndrome,' where people sitting next to each other feel free to talk candidly about their lives to strangers they'll never see again. European tours are much the same. I'm sure they'll be eager to unburden themselves to you."

Ali stood up and brushed the snow off the seat of her pants. "Okay, tell me about André."

"All right. That charismatic man over there—with the red baseball cap—is the tour guide, André Le Grand. He's a French national and makes his living leading tours through Europe. Now he is very good as a tour guide, but he's also what you would call a 'Don Juan.' You see, Ali, on every tour he chooses two or three women, and they become his lovers, or one might say his 'marks.' He convinces each woman that she is the chosen one for this tour."

"But how does he pull that off, if he chooses more than one?"

"He explains that intimacy with clients is strictly prohibited by the tour company, so he asks them to keep the affair secret. For a lonely woman looking for romance in Europe, what could be more enticing? His current conquests are a mother and daughter hoping to patch up their wounded relationship on the tour. Ali, I'd like you to get to know them. The mother is Dorothy, the daughter is Cassie. I'll point them out to you. But I want to impress upon you that we are observing only, not interfering. And also, Ali, I suggest you try to be as non-judgmental as possible. Is that clear?"

Ali said it was, and had her first opportunity to meet up with Dorothy when they stopped for lunch in a '50s retro-style cafeteria, conspicuously out of place at the top of the pristine ski slope. Vio pointed Dorothy out. She was standing alone in the cafeteria line, pushing her tray along the metal track, eyeing the food choices as she moved along, turning periodically to scan the dining room. As Dorothy returned her attention to the line, she grabbed a coffee cup, a sandwich and some chocolate pudding, and moved along to the coffee machine. Ali took a tray and met her there.

"I hope the coffee is as good here as it is in France," Ali said to start up a conversation. Coffee always seemed to be a good ice breaker.

"I hear you," replied Dorothy. We didn't see you in Paris. Did you just join the tour?" Before Ali could answer, Dorothy followed with the question, "Are you alone?"

Ali had to think fast, remembering that Vio was visible only to her, so she was essentially alone. "Yes, I'm traveling by myself. My name is Alicia Morgenstern, but you can call me Ali. I'm from New York. How about you?"

"I'm here with my daughter Cassie. I'm Dorothy. Cassie is recently divorced, so I thought I'd take her with me and do a mother/daughter thing, you know."

By this time, they had both filled their coffee cups and their trays had reached the end of the track. They both pulled out their wallets to pay. Dorothy looked around the room once more, sighed, and then pointed to a small Formica table by the window. "Would you like to join me? I don't see Cassie anywhere, and I'd enjoy the company."

"Thank you. I'd love to hear more about you both."

It didn't take long for Dorothy to start in with her story, just as Vio had predicted.

"Yes, it's hard being a mother. I used to sing, you know, in front of a big band. And I think I might have become famous if it weren't for that little indiscretion." She looked at Ali, who nodded to let her know she understood the innuendo. "So, even though Cassie's father was gone the next day—to God knows where—when I found out I was pregnant, I decided to keep the kid. I didn't know how hard it would be. I gave up everything for her. . . I wonder where she is. She has to eat . . . I've had men in my life, but they all seemed to be unavailable types. Now that I'm fifty . . ." She waited for Ali to deny that she looked anywhere near fifty, which Ali did on cue.

"You're kidding me. You don't look a day over thirty-five."

"It's not so easy anymore. There are so many young girls who make themselves available, you know." Ali nodded in agreement, and Dorothy continued. "I've certainly had my ups and downs with men. I'm glad my daughter has always been there. She's always been so strong for me. I don't know what I'd do without her. Now she's going through a divorce, and with two small kids. I really can relate to what she's going through, being a single mother myself."

Ali wondered if Dorothy would mention anything about André. They talked all the way through dessert with no mention of him, and Ali followed Vio's instruction of non-interference.

After lunch, Ali excused herself. She still had the interview with Cassie, if she could locate her. As Ali walked into the small souvenir shop, Vio pointed out Cassie at the watch counter.

Ali initiated the conversation. "Bringing home a Swiss watch as a souvenir? I'm thinking of one too. I like the ones with two faces." Ali wondered if that was a Freudian slip.

"Hey, cool. So while you're in Europe you can keep track of the time at home. I'm looking for a gift for a special someone. I'm Cassie. I haven't seen you on the tour before, have I? Where are you from?"

"I'm Ali, from New York, Manhattan. How about you?"

"Kansas, Wichita, Kansas. I'm here with my mother." Cassie turned her attention to the saleswoman behind the counter. "Can I see that watch there? Yes, that one."

"Oh, I see, a mother and daughter trip. Sounds nice —"

"I wish. No, we don't get along too well. But I don't want to burden you with the details." She tried on the watch, although judging by its size, it was for a man. "Yes, I'll take this one. Could you please gift wrap it for me?"

Ali chose the "two-faced" watch, thinking it would provide a chuckle or two when she got back home. By the time they both had completed their purchases, they were on their way to becoming friends.

"Oh God, there's my mom over there." Cassie discretely tilted her head toward the postcard display, where her mother was slowly spinning the circular rack. "I was able to elude her at lunchtime by skipping the meal completely, but now she's watching me from behind that display. She just can't leave me alone for a minute. I'm so grateful the guide, André, got us separate rooms, even though we paid for double occupancy. You know, since I was a little girl, she's always depended on me. You'd think a child should be able to depend on her mom, but no, not in our family. Now I know, since my divorce, that being a single mother is a huge task, but I'm handling it all right. My mom, though, she'd get involved with all these men, and then, when they'd leave her, I was stuck with a basket case for a mother. When do I get my turn? Now I'm a mom, and again others are still depending on me." She stopped for a moment, to catch her breath and see if Ali was showing any interest. "I'm so sorry. I'm really dumping on you."

"No, not at all. I haven't had much luck with men either. Have you dated since your divorce?"

"Not much. No time for that. There is a guy here on the tour I'm kind of interested in though."

She didn't give any other details, and Ali knew it wasn't her job to probe.

"Well, Cassie, good luck with that. I think I'll bring my purchases back to my room now. No sense carting them around. I'll see you later on, okay?"

"Okay, thanks for listening. I feel a lot better."

Ali went back toward the shuttle to the hotel. Since she didn't really have a room, she waited for Vio to meet her there, which, of course, she did.

"What have you learned, Ali?" Vio asked.

"I got the histories from both of them. Although they both have victim stories about their relationship, they seem relatively happy here on the tour."

"Good work. So what have you decided about them and their situation thus far?"

"Well, everyone seems to be happy, at least for the moment. I think they both know that this type of affair ends at the conclusion of the tour. I have to admit I secretly hope that neither of them finds out about the other and that they go home with lovely memories."

"Ali, I didn't know you were a romantic."

"I can't imagine a happier ending in these circumstances. Can you?"

Violetta just smiled.

The next time Ali saw Cassie and Dorothy, they were sitting together on a blanket on the snow, looking out on the beautiful turquoise lake. They each seemed to be in total bliss. They reminded Ali of how she had felt when she first fell in love with Johan. Her heart was wide open, the colors of nature were more intense, and she heard music everywhere. She watched the two women, swaying gently to the music in their hearts, as they saw a small rowboat come into view. Dorothy turned to Cassie and said, "Look at that lovely little boat on the lake. How romantic. Wouldn't it be delightful to be in a rowboat, floating on the lake with someone you love?"

"Oh yes, that would be too wonderful even to imagine." They both closed their eyes, returning to their daydreams, now with the image of themselves and André, in a boat on a pristine alpine lake.

Cassie was the first to notice, as she opened her eyes. "Mom, that's André in the boat, isn't it?"

"Yes, Dear. I recognize him by his cute red baseball hat." At first André's presence seemed to blend nicely with their fantasies, but as the boat came closer to the shore, Cassie sat up and squinted to get a better look.

"Mom, isn't that a woman moving over to sit next to him?"

Dorothy, already sitting up, tilted her head, thought for a moment, and then responded, "Oh yes, that must be Maria. She's a local tour guide, joining the group to show us Lucerne. Remember he told us about her yesterday? They're probably discussing the tour."

"Oh yes, I remember." Cassie was noticeably relieved.

Ali looked at the two women, as André and Maria lifted their oars from the water and placed them inside the boat. As the boat began to float, the two figures seemed to merge into one. The women on the shore stared for a moment, their faces showing identical expressions of disbelief at first, and then jealous rage. They simultaneously shouted out, "No! He's mine!"

"Mom, what are you talking about?"

"Cassie, where do you think I've been these last three out of five past nights? Did you really believe that I wanted to walk alone in the evening moonlight?"

"Well, where do you think I was on those other two nights?"

Dorothy reflected back on the day they arrived in Paris and André had generously offered to pull some strings and get them private rooms. "He's planned this from the beginning. Oh, my God!"

In the middle of the beautiful mountain lake, in a rowboat drifting slowly toward the shore, André and Maria finally released their embrace.

André spoke first. "Maria, it's so wonderful to be with you again, here in this beautiful country. You make my tours in Switzerland so sweet."

She kissed him gently on the forehead. "André, I've counted the days . . . I'm so glad to see you again."

They continued to look lovingly at each other as they moved to their sides of the boat, picked up their oars and replaced them in the oar locks.

As they maneuvered the boat around to face the shore, André's gaze fell upon two figures slowly leaning forward and staring at him in disbelief. It was undeniable that these women were his conquests of the previous week, and he knew his deception had been exposed. The two women fell back on their blanket and remained there for quite a while. But as the boat came closer to the shore, he was confused by what he saw. The mother and daughter, at odds with each other from the first day, were rolling together in the snow like children, laughing, screaming, crying and embracing.

Ali and Vio were still watching from a distance and saw the same scene. "Vio, what just happened?"

"Would you like to know? I'll show you."

Ali found herself moving into the consciousness of Cassie. The first thought she had was *I hope the boat sinks.* Ali had no problem empathizing with that. Then Cassie went over in her mind all the compliments and lies that she had so willingly believed, just to feel attractive and special. She knew the affair would be short-lived, but had decided to be wild for once, as her mother had been. She could see now that it was empty and futile, and it left a gnawing hole in her heart. Cassie reached into her pocket and wrapped her fingers around the rectangular box holding the watch she had so lovingly purchased for André in the gift shop. The feeling that Ali sensed in Cassie's chest was like a deflated balloon and the thought she heard was, *I will never find love, never.*

Ali's awareness moved then into the consciousness of Dorothy, who also wished the boat would sink. How could she have fallen for that line, with his compliments about the attractiveness of an older woman. And who was her competition? Her own daughter. Her feelings were a mixture of anger and shame. She looked at her daughter, recognized her pain, and wished that there was something she could do to fill the hole. But how could she help her daughter fill the empty hole in her heart, when her own heart was empty? *There is no love in the world, not for me, not for Cassie, not for anyone. It's hopeless.*

Ali then sensed a gnawing, empty space in her stomach as she moved deeper into her own feelings of loneliness and despair. The feeling was too familiar, and Ali, at first, resisted going further, but the pain of the resistance became unbearable, so she let go. She found herself again falling, deeper and deeper, into a dark abyss. It was so dark and so deep, she feared the falling would never end, and she feared it would end in the total annihilation of her being.

In the last moment, when all hope was gone, she felt herself being caught and cradled in the huge arms of a soft and loving feminine presence. She felt totally vulnerable and, at the same time, totally safe. All her feelings of loneliness, desperation and fear dissolved in this all-encompassing Love. After what seemed like hours, but was only a few minutes, Ali turned her attention to Cassie and Dorothy, and recognized that they were sharing the same experience. She saw them both lying down in the snow, held in the arms of a huge angel who cradled not only them, but the entire world.

After some time, the two women, satiated with this feeling of Love, sat up and faced each other. Both were vulnerable and full at the same time. Their hearts were wide open. Ali could see and feel tremendous love energy moving through them and between them. When it became too powerful for them to contain, they both fell back in the snow, and started rolling around with total abandon. She knew they didn't feel the cold or the dampness. They were radiating incredible heat and light. And then she saw them merge with the pristine beauty of the mountains, the lake, the snow, and the rosy glow of sunset. Ali could feel it too. And what she felt she could only later describe as what it was to know herself, to truly know herself, as Love, the Lover and the Beloved, as One.

Vio stood by, allowing Ali to bathe in Love for a time, and then when the moment was right, she gently put her arm around Ali's shoulders and whispered, "There is much to learn and experience in the realm of Divine Love. I think that for today you've had a good taste. I promise there will be more to come."

As Ali drove home, she wondered if she could possibly stand that much love.

6
Florida

While Ali was eating her breakfast, thinking about where Violetta might take her that day, her first thought was *Florida*. Her second thought was, *No, not Florida! That's the place where New Yorkers go to die and Cubans go to escape Castro.* She decided not to mention Florida to Violetta. She thought maybe Egypt, Istanbul or Japan would be exciting destinations for today's journey.

By the time Ali had completed her drive to Rose Cottage, she was determined that today's trip would have to be some place exotic. She sat herself down at the kitchen table, cupped her hands around the now familiar cup of coffee, and made her suggestion. "I had an intuition when I first woke up. . ." Ali hesitated, since she didn't want to give Vio any ideas. "Well, on second thought, maybe Egypt or Japan, Istanbul . . ." Violetta smiled, and Ali knew, in that moment, that they were going to Florida.

"Ali, let me tell you about second thoughts. The idea of Florida. . . it was Florida, wasn't it? The first idea was not your thought, it was your direction. The second thought was really your first thought. A bit of advice I'd like to give you is—unless it feels impulsive or fearful—trust the first thought."

"Even if I don't want to do it?"

"*Especially* if you don't want to do it. Your guides give you direction always on what you call the first thought; your ego is usually the author of the second. To prove it, we will go to Florida today, and you will see the value of following the first thought. And no need for a bathing suit or sunscreen on this trip."

"Have you ever been to Florida, Vio?" Ali stood up, expecting a simple response, and began preparing herself for the now familiar transport to the day's destination.

"Not in this lifetime, but I have many friends there. I'm taking you today to meet a very special friend. I call her 'Lovely Annette.'"

That sounded like a riddle to Ali, but she decided to wait and see, rather than annoy Vio with too many questions.

As Vio predicted, the beautiful blue Atlantic Ocean eluded them, as they made their entrance through the ceiling of a retirement community into the hallway outside apartment 423.

This particular community was three-tiered, which meant that it included independent living, assisted living—with or without memory care—and a hospital, all on the same site. The door was open, and Ali watched from the hallway as one of the family members—most likely the daughter—was packing her mother's clothing while another family member was trying, along with some of the staff, to explain to the elderly woman that she was moving to an apartment in the memory unit, but her husband would remain where he was. Sometimes she seemed alert enough to understand what was happening, and then in the next moment she was confused, not knowing who her husband was or where these strangers were intending to take her.

The family members, believing that Ali was part of the staff, invited her to participate and were confiding in her their emotions regarding the move. They had hoped they were incorrect in their perception, but they admitted that the woman they knew and loved was slowly but surely leaving them. The body that was living in this apartment and eating meals, bore little resemblance to the woman who had raised them, read them fairytales, made Christmas dinner and held the grandchildren and great-grandchildren on her lap. Now she often wasn't even able to recognize who they were.

The daughter confided in Ali that her mother had recently been preparing extra food for dinner. Ali didn't find that to be a reason to make a diagnosis, until the daughter took Ali by the arm and walked her into the kitchen, where her mother was setting the table for four.

"Mom, who are those extra settings for?"

"Oh, dear, didn't I tell you about the two children who come by sometimes? I make sure I always have the table set so they will feel welcomed."

"Do they ever eat anything?"

"Not much, dear. They don't have big appetites. But I very much enjoy their visit."

"Are these the children, Mom?" she asked, as she pointed to the grandchildren, who were occupied with their hand-held computers, trying to stay out of the way.

"Oh no, don't be silly. I don't know those children. Who are they? What are they doing in my house?"

Ali's heart sank. Although she didn't have to deal with aging issues with her own parents, she was not unfamiliar with the threat of Alzheimer's or dementia for her generation.

Ali excused herself for a moment and walked into the hall so that she could speak to Vio in private without appearing schizophrenic to the family.

"If you remember, Ali, I told you I had Alzheimer's disease myself. My son and his wife were so distressed by the situation, they washed their hands of me. I finished my days in a nursing home, not as lovely as this one, but at that point I really didn't care at all about my physical surroundings. You see my body did what it needed to do with the part of my brain that still functioned on the physical level, while the other parts of my brain, which hadn't been utilized here in this dimension, were activated. So even though I looked, on the outside, to be mentally and physically disabled, my spirit was finally free to soar."

"I don't understand how that could be." Ali responded.

"Don't you really mean you don't believe me?"

"I don't believe you—which is odd, because I couldn't be here in Florida right now without suspending my beliefs. But what you just said is way beyond any belief systems I hold—even beyond that you can bend time and space."

"I know. Thinking outside the body is a new concept for you, but since you've signed up for the course, I'm delighted to share it with you. Perhaps then you will be able to release another major fear of yours. This woman is 'Lovely Annette.' I've been visiting her recently. The more she has been leaving the reality of Florida, the more she has been able to see me. Just last week, right before you and I met, she invited me to dinner to meet the children. And they were just delightful."

"Were the children real on your dimension, or were they her children who died?"

"Yes, to the first question, and the answer to the second is that they are not really children; they are spirit guides that have come to her in a form she can most readily accept. They allow her to continue to give—which is something she is unable to do in her physical and mental condition—and so they appear as children. I come to her as a friend who, having had the same experience as she, can explain to her what is happening, much as I am doing for you, but under different circumstances."

"Did you have help like this when you had Alzheimer's disease?"

"Of course, everyone does. You think about divine intervention, or angels as coming to you if you pray. Some of this is correct, but a little tweak can explain it more intelligibly for you. Angels and guides, or however you would like to describe them, are all around you all the time, in another dimension—but that dimension is not in another place, it is just on another vibratory level. It's like a dog who can hear a whistle you cannot hear, but the whistle is not in another location. You just don't have the ability to hear it. In times of extreme stress or grief or pain, the chemicals in the body actually change and allow you to use brain receptors that are made only for certain tasks. When people have Alzheimer's disease, the one system closes down, intermittently or permanently, and the body goes on automatic pilot, you might say. The other parts of the brain, freed from all the details of life, the judgments, the complaints, the goals, the decisions, are now able to see what is always there and to access others consciously from other dimensions."

"Does that happen in spiritual practices as well?"

"Yes, certainly it does. Or it can just happen by Grace."

"So what are you teaching Lovely Annette?"

"It's not so much teaching as being a guide and letting her know that it is all okay."

"Can I speak to her?"

"I'll ask her if she'd like to speak to you. We'll have to provide a location where you won't be overheard."

Vio entered the apartment through the door and Ali followed. They both walked into the small kitchen area, unnoticed by the family, where they could be alone with Annette.

"Yes, she said she'd love to be of assistance, and perhaps you can tell her family that she is well. But you'll need to couch it in terms that will not frighten them. I don't think they would be amenable to hearing a discussion like this. Remember how long it took before you even sipped the coffee. Let me bring her over to you."

The elderly woman in the kitchen continued to set the table, while another younger-looking body, as translucent as Violetta, glided over to Ali and extended her hand.

"Hello, I'm Annette. I'm very glad you are visiting me here today. My family is concerned that they have lost me—and indeed they have. They are talking to the body as if it were me, and in that case, I am lost, almost totally. I can come in periodically, and they rejoice in those moments, but those are moments of great difficulty for me, like squeezing a foot into a tight shoe."

"But after a whole life, doesn't your family mean anything to you?" Ali asked.

"I hope this is not upsetting to you, child, but I can't remember the part of me that fretted over the report cards of my children, worried over their marital choices, or was critical of their housekeeping. I actually wouldn't know these details had they not thought of them in my presence. They still hold a lot of resentments, even though they say I was a fine mother. That's just how it goes; you can't please everyone, now can you? Everything you teach a child takes away their freedom and their innocence, but you must do it to prepare them for life in the world. And all the while, you love them more than you can ever say. What a thankless task the role of the parent is!"

"It's so sad to see your children unable to know how wonderfully wise and happy you are. Is there a way we could show them or tell them?"

"Of course you can try. But—as Violetta knows—they won't understand, and you will only lose your credibility with them. When they are ready, they will be open to the contact I have with them all the time. You see, even though I don't place importance on remembering the details of our relationship on the earth dimension, I know they are caring for my body, and I love them for it. If I can be of assistance, I will; but I have no control over what the body does and says—and that is something I'm still getting used to."

"I remember that experience myself," Ali recounted. "I was having a wisdom tooth pulled and they gave me nitrous oxide, or laughing gas. Before long I was up on the ceiling watching the dentist working on me. I could see myself, and I even noticed I was fully clothed and watching from the ceiling. I wonder who it was that noticed that? At one point the dentist asked me a question (the 'me' in the chair) and I remember saying to myself, 'I wonder if she'll answer.' And, believe it or not, she did. Is it like that for you also?"

"That is an excellent description. That is exactly my experience." Annette replied.

"How do you feel about your husband living alone now?"

"Ah, I'm glad you asked. I am able to contact him because of our long time together. Since he is not a believer in other dimensions, and Vio is not able to coach him at this time, he can see me only in his dreams—some he remembers and others he doesn't. I do visit him and make sure he is okay, but again, my love for him is no different from my love for everyone and everything."

"Tell me more about that. It seems like less love, because it's not directed to one person—even the person you've been married to for over fifty years."

"I'm sensing this is a sensitive issue for you. Am I correct?" Annette asked.

"Yes. I'd like to think I am special to people I know in my life. What you're expressing is sort of saying that no one is more special than anyone else when you get to the 'other side.' Do you love the mailman as much as your husband?" asked Ali.

"These are the types of issues that don't translate well from one state to another. Is individual love stronger than all-encompassing radiant love?"

"Yes. I think so. I remember in the days of the 'Haight-Ashbury' in San Francisco, the 'Summer of Love,' when people thought they were expressing God's love, unconditionally, and a lot of women ended up as single parents."

"I can answer this one," Violetta interceded. "This is a big problem, especially among the Baby Boomers. Your generation, Ali, either through experimentation with meditation techniques or sometimes drugs, had experiences of love with a capital 'L.' But without the understanding of how to move between levels, and how to bring higher consciousness down onto the earth plane, there were some casualties. Now you are learning how to bring spiritual awareness into everyday life without inappropriately expecting behavior from the higher planes in the denser planes."

"Can you elaborate on that, Vio? What am I learning?"

"No, Ali. What you are learning will come through experience, not lectures. Stick around, and you'll see what I mean. I will tell you that one mistake that is often made by those who glimpse a higher level of reality—and there are levels beyond those you have ever experienced as well—is that they mistakenly denigrate the denser levels. It's as absurd as a high school student thinking that first graders are stupid. Does that make sense to you?"

"Of course, you can't judge one grade by another grade's standards. I never thought of it that way before."

"That's correct. And you will find—when you see from the higher dimension—that there isn't any need to judge, change or even teach anyone."

"But aren't you teaching me?"

"When you see who *you* really are, you'll see the absurdity of that perception."

"I look forward to that."

"Sorry, Ali. Ali will never see that."

"Is that a paradox, Vio?"

"That could very well be."

Ali tried to make sense out of what was just said, but then decided to save it for another time. She looked back at Violetta and Lovely Annette, arm in arm, and smiled. "I think that's enough for my little mind right now. Annette, it was lovely meeting you. I guess that's why Vio called you 'Lovely Annette.' I don't think I'll ever think about Alzheimer's patients the same way again."

Vio and Annette simultaneously chimed in, "It's not just Alzheimer's patients. It's everyone!"

Just before leaving, Ali toyed with the idea of trying to explain all this to Annette's family, but with the momentary ability to see through her eyes, or the eyes of Love, she knew they would be fine and in time would learn what they needed to know.

The next moment found Ali and Vio sitting on the porch swing of Rose Cottage.

"Thank you for a wonderful visit." Ali said to Vio. "I hope I never forget the teachings I received today."

"Never worry about forgetting or remembering the Truth. It is there beyond thought, always. It is not just available to you; it is what you are. It can never be lost. I'll see you tomorrow."

7

The Loft

Saturday morning, Ali awoke and began, as she did each morning, to remember who and where she was, what there was to be worried about, and what there was to be happy about—unfortunately in that order. This morning, gratefully, she realized there really wasn't anything to worry about. She sat up in bed, and said to herself, *I have everything I ever wanted, and more. My God, life is magnificent!*

Just as she finished thinking those words, a nagging "inner voice"—not unfamiliar to her—challenged her declaration. *But this apartment is so far away from the action. Wouldn't you rather live in a loft in Chelsea?*

Now that's not very spiritual . . . Ali thought. *I have an apartment on the Upper East Side of Manhattan, a house at Blue Swan Lake, and a spirit guide teaching me to move between dimensions. What else could I possibly ask for?*

The inner voice responded, *How about a loft in Chelsea? You could ask her for that. Then you'd really have everything.*

Ali responded with what she referred to as her "spiritual inner voice," *I don't want anything else. I'm fulfilled. I don't need possessions anymore. And I know who you are. You're the voice of temptation, and I'm not falling for your games.*

Ali's inner conversation continued, but remained unresolved during her drive to the lake house. As she pulled up in the driveway, she was determined to put the whole issue of desire out of her mind. She was ashamed of herself that she had let it go on so long. She rang the bell and turned the key in the lock. As she pushed open the door Violetta called to her, inviting her into the kitchen.

"Ali, I sense you're not 100% here. What happened this morning? Where has your mind taken you today?" Violetta asked, as she gestured toward the now familiar coffee cup.

Ali realized she couldn't hide anything from Violetta. "I'm really embarrassed to tell you this. I know I should be free of desire, especially now—when I'm learning so much from you about the different dimensions—but I have a desire about living in a loft in Chelsea . . ." her eyes glazed over, "maybe over an art gallery or a boutique, with floor to ceiling windows and exposed ductwork . . . and that voice just won't leave me alone. I wish you could help me put it out of my mind and move on to more important things."

"The mind is intriguing, isn't it, Ali? Then how are we to determine which thoughts or desires are spiritual and which are material? And will the mind ever stop desiring?"

Ali was eager to hear more about this subject, but Violetta surprised her by reaching into the pocket of her apron and pulling out a key ring with two keys. "Apartment 5B. I can show you a nice loft on Fifth Avenue near Eighteenth Street, in the Chelsea District of Manhattan, I believe." She glanced at the keys, saying, "Yes, 5B, that's the one. Shall we go?"

Ali knew by now that questioning Violetta's suggestions was pointless, so she lifted her cup, took another mouthful, and nodded her head.

Before she could finish swallowing her coffee, Ali found herself standing at the door of Apartment 5B. Vio unlocked the door and invited her inside. Ali saw that it was one huge room with high ceilings and exposed ducts. The small but very modern kitchen was on the left as she walked in, with the very popular concrete countertops, green glass tiles and stainless steel appliances. The view directly ahead was floor to ceiling windows that offered a wide view of Fifth Avenue. It was furnished with modern, minimalist furniture—very fashionable and appropriate for the district. There was a nook against a brick wall on the left, set up as an office and reading area, with a comfortable chair, a gas fireplace, and floor to ceiling bookshelves. Another area, partially hidden behind rice paper shoji screens, was set aside for sleeping. Ali couldn't believe her eyes. It was perfect, exactly as she had imagined it. "This is wonderful! Are you offering this to me?"

"How does it feel? Does it fulfill your desire?"

"Oh yes, Vio!"

"Well then, how could I refuse?" Vio placed the keys in Ali's waiting hands. Ali closed her eyes and cradled them, as if she were holding a sacred object, before putting them in her purse.

"Thanks so much. But I have one lingering question. I've read that houses with glass walls opposite the front door are not good design according to *Feng Shui*. It said something about the energy going right out the window. But I feel so drawn to this type of living. How do you feel about this, Violetta?"

"You're asking me what *my* feelings are about this?"

"Oh, I mean, what do *you* believe?"

"What do *I* believe?"

"Are you teasing me?" Ali was feeling a bit exasperated by this *Zen* method of conversation. She really wanted to know if it was okay to want to live there.

"What do *you* believe, Ali? Can energy be lost?"

"I don't know."

"Well, if you think energy can be lost, then it can. Do you know why you long to live in a loft?"

"Because it's chic?"

"Maybe that's one reason. What about your deeper feelings? How does your spirit feel in the loft? Go to the place of your Truth, not your mind, and tell me how your Spirit feels."

Ali took a moment to reflect. "Ah . . . my Spirit loves the windows and not because of the view exactly. I don't know how to describe it, but it seems as if my Spirit longs for transparency." She wasn't sure where that phrase came from, but was pleased when she heard herself say it.

"Very beautifully put. For you, this is true. So now that your Spirit is communicating with you, why don't you ask if energy can be lost?"

Ali again reflected, placing her attention between and behind her eyes. "My Spirit is one with energy. It can never be lost."

"Very good. I'm going to ask you to reflect this way when you have questions for me, because you have the very best answers within yourself. So now, Ali, I'll ask you how it feels to be totally fulfilled."

"It feels so freeing. There's nothing more that I want. There's a feeling like I can rest now. That nagging inner voice is finally quiet." But Ali still seemed confused. Her original question had been about desire, and yet Vio's response had been to satisfy her desire. That was certainly not what she had expected.

"Vio, I've always heard that the less you have, the better. Didn't Jesus say it was hard for a rich man to enter the kingdom of heaven? And then there's the story of Buddha, begging for his food. But here I am in this beautiful loft. Is this going to hamper my progress and my learning with you?"

"Ali, this is an interesting question because it brings up a whole gamut of beliefs you will find in spiritual trainings of all sorts. I'm going to tell you that nothing you believe about what is 'spiritual' is true. You cannot go by any opinions of anyone who has gone before. Many have achieved 'Enlightenment,' and they don't know how—so they look back on what they did in the past, and assume that the cause and effect of their actions brought them to that moment. Maybe they beat themselves and starved themselves and denied themselves every pleasure, and then, in one moment woke up. Do they know how that happened? What if God just thought they were being ridiculous, and said, 'Enough of this, already!' Ali, of course I'm joking, but what holds you back from knowing your True Self is only the belief that there's something you must do. You've studied so many systems, and if you add up all the austerities and all the practices, you could be busy your whole life chanting, fasting, and living in a cave. And do you know what you would be left with?"

"The desire to give up everything?"

"Yes. What else?"

"The belief that this will get me to my goal?"

"Yes, again. And the belief that your goal is not already achieved."

"So it's okay to live in a loft in Chelsea?"

"Didn't your Spirit just tell you it enjoyed the transparency of this place? That it felt good here?"

"Yes, but —"

"But what else can you possibly go on other than what feels good to you? What felt good to somebody else four hundred years ago in Tibet, or two thousand years ago in Jerusalem or China, probably won't work for you, and is more likely to drive you crazy."

"Are you really saying forget everything I've learned? What about all the practices I've done to be able to move healing energy around? It does help people, doesn't it?" Ali walked toward one of the bookcase, recognizing her own collection already on the shelves. "Vio, these are my books, aren't they?"

"Yes Ali. You'll find I've moved your possessions here. I knew you'd want to stay."

"Okay, I guess I shouldn't be surprised. But look at all these books I've collected and read over the years. If what you're saying is true, then what's the point of them?"

"There is nothing wrong with learning mastery, Ali. For example, you studied dance. You just couldn't start jumping around and be a ballet dancer, even if you were inspired. You still had to master the form. But mastery is not what we're doing here; we're doing something entirely different.

"In addition, Ali, there's nothing wrong with enjoying books or living in a pleasant environment, sitting in a comfortable chair, or having good friends. But just don't make the seeking of them your occupation. Don't make the seeking of *anything* your occupation. You then can enjoy them—but remembering always who you are. You are not the one with desires."

"Who is the one with desires?" Ali was even more confused.

"Ask your Spirit, Ali."

"My Spirit desires only to be known." She shocked herself again when she said that. "So, who wanted the loft, or anything else, for that matter?"

"Ali, remember what I taught you about how the mind makes a picture to match a feeling? For example, while you are dreaming, the phone in your bedroom rings. The dream imagery somehow might incorporate the phone ringing into your dream as perhaps a huge bell in a cathedral. That's what the mind does. Do you follow this so far?"

"Yes, I'm with you. The most obvious explanation of that is when I have to go to the bathroom while I'm asleep, and that is incorporated in the dream." She wondered if that was a bit over-the-top for Vio, who just smiled, and continued.

"Okay, Ali. So, similarly, an impulse of the Spirit might be interpreted by the subconscious mind in a more literal way.

What the Spirit might experience as the void or emptiness, the ego might interpret as a hole that needs filling, or a thirst that can't be satisfied. If you're alone, you might say you want a partner, if you're in a relationship, you might desire to be alone. If you're childless, you might think a family would fulfill you, and then when you have a child and a family, again you might desire freedom. You have an apartment, and then you want a loft. Do you see how it all comes from one desire, Ali?"

"So, what's the point, then, in getting rid of material things, if the desire will always remain?"

"A good observation. No matter how much you pare down, it's always something. Now you know what that something is."

"So now that I know, I can just relax and embrace the Spirit, because that's what she really wants—for me to know her, to be her. Is that right?"

"Is that right, Ali?"

"Yes. Now what?"

"Well, you have a lot of arranging to do. As you have seen, I've moved all your possessions to the new apartment. You'll have to deliver your old keys to your landlord and turn on the utilities, but everything else is already arranged for you, and the deed is on the desk. So, I'll see you tomorrow morning at the lake house. In the meantime, enjoy your new home." And at that moment, Vio disappeared from view.

Ali walked back over to her new desk, and noticed a book she hadn't seen before. The title was *The Essential Rumi, translated by Coleman Barks*. The book fell open to page 17, *The Reed Flute's Song*. She read it with her heart as well as her eyes:

THE REED FLUTE'S SONG

>Listen to the story told by the reed,
>of being separated.
>
>"Since I was cut from the reedbed,
>I have made this crying sound.
>
>Anyone apart from someone he loves
>understands what I say.
>
>Anyone pulled from a source
>longs to go back.
>
>At any gathering, I am there,
>mingling in the laughing and grieving,
>
>A friend to each, but few
>will hear the secrets hidden
>
>within the notes. No ears for that.
>Body flowing out of spirit,
>
>Spirit up from body: no concealing
>that mixing. But it's not given us
>
>to see the soul. The reed flute
>is fire, not wind. Be that empty."
>
>Hear the love fire tangled
>in the reed notes, as bewilderment

The Legacy of Violetta Rose

melts into wine. The reed is a friend
to all who want the fabric torn

and drawn away. The reed is hurt
and salve combining. Intimacy

and longing for intimacy, one
song. A disastrous surrender

and a fine love, together. The one
who secretly hears this is senseless.

A tongue has one customer, the ear.
A sugarcane flute has such effect

because it was able to make sugar
in the reedbed. The sound it makes

is for everyone. Days full of wanting,
let them go by without worrying

that they do. Stay where you are
inside such a pure, hollow note.

Every thirst gets satisfied except
that of these fish, the mystics,

who swim a vast ocean of grace
still somehow longing for it!

No one lives in that without
being nourished every day.

But if someone doesn't want to hear
the song of the reed flute,

it's best to cut conversation
short, say good-bye, and leave.

The poem spoke of the song of the flute, and how its crying sound was the cry of separation from the reedbed. As Ali read the poem, she wanted to sob. As she released the tears she saw—in her mind's eye—all the people and situations that she felt had caused her pain: the loss of her parents, the broken engagement, childhood friends rejecting her, being treated unfairly at school . . . all these memories, and many more, filled the space. Next, Ali found herself moving backwards in time, and all the feelings converged into the one cry. It was the cry of the newborn baby, the pain of separation from the source. And in the sobbing and the realization, she fell deeply asleep.

8

Sedona, Arizona

It was Sunday, and for the first time Ali woke up in her new downtown loft. Since she was eager to return to see Violetta, she powered up her laptop and did a quick map search. She found that the new directions to Blue Swan Lake still routed her through the Lincoln Tunnel, but with an estimated traveling time ten minutes shorter than the trip from uptown—although the time gained seemed irrelevant, since she still could not recall the ride after entering the tunnel anyway. Nevertheless, one hour and fifty minutes later—by her watch at least—she was back in the kitchen of Rose Cottage, sitting across from Violetta, who was sipping tea.

A medium-sized white dog, with soulful eyes and long floppy ears, scampered across the room and licked Ali's hand. "Who is this? Is this your dog?"

"This, my dear, is Layla. She's a Wheaten Terrier. She was my dog many years ago, and has returned for our delight and to join us on our adventures."

"Is she invisible to others, as you are?"

"You could say she is a 'multi-dimensional' dog. She has the special ability of being visible or invisible on either plane. She knows when it's appropriate to appear and disappear. You'll see." Layla seemed very happy to be back with her mistress and eager to be of service. Ali shared many of these same feelings about Violetta, and enjoyed the addition of the dog's energy.

Even before Ali could inquire about their destination, all three of them were moving through space, and landed at a table in the lobby of a large, luxurious hotel (Ali was visible, but Layla and Vio remained in spirit form). A uniformed doorman approached their table. His name tag said "John—Honolulu." He welcomed Ali, and then reached into his pocket. "You know, we are dog friendly here at this hotel." he said, as he opened his hand to reveal a biscuit for Layla—who took the cue and manifested beside him.

Ali tried to make sense of what she had just seen, but before she had a chance to ask, she saw Vio (still in spirit form) approaching the doorman.

"John, it's good to see you again."

"Wonderful to see you too, Violetta."

"Are we in Honolulu?" Ali asked, trying not to intrude, but eager to know where she was.

"No, you're in Scottsdale, Arizona, and I have a wonderful tour set up for you that I know you'll all enjoy."

Ali needed an explanation, and since there was no one else within earshot, Vio explained. "John is a friend I meet on the other dimensions. He has work here to do on Earth, and I run into him periodically on both planes. I thought you might like to meet him. Did I explain it well enough for you, John?"

"Yes, Violetta. I envy that you can live now solely on the higher planes. It gets really hot here in the summers, you know. Maybe someday I'll graduate and see you over there."

"John, you know you're on special assignment. Opening doors should never be underestimated. It's the greatest work there is."

Ali watched as Layla jumped up and licked his face. "Layla seems to know him."

"Oh yes, they're old friends. They're both happy to see each other, as you can probably tell."

John patted Layla and told her to sit. "Let's go over to the concierge, and she can explain the tour. Layla, I think you'll need to be invisible on this one—but I know you and Vio will enjoy it in your own way."

John and Ali (with Layla and Vio in spirit form) walked over to the Concierge Desk. John whispered to Marlene, "I think this visitor would very much enjoy a jeep tour of Sedona. Could you please tell her about it?"

"I'd be happy to, John." She handed Ali a brochure and invited her to have a seat at her desk. "One of the side trips that we recommend to our guests is a visit to Sedona. It's only about two and a half hours from here, but the terrain is entirely different, with beautiful red rock canyons and unique geological formations. The area was sacred to the Indians almost a thousand years ago, and some people even today believe it has special energy. Many of our guests tell me it's the most inspiring and beautiful place they've ever seen."

"Thank you. I'd love to see Sedona; it sounds wonderful." Ali followed John as he led the way through the lobby to the main entrance. When the automatic glass doors opened, they stepped through, finding themselves, not in the driveway of a Scottsdale hotel, but in front of a small kiosk nestled between the walls of a beautiful red rock canyon in Sedona.

Inside the kiosk was an old hippie with long gray hair pulled back with a leather tie. He wore a well seasoned cowboy hat and a necklace of turquoise beads. "Good morning. Can I interest you in a jeep tour of the sacred energy vortexes of Sedona?" he asked.

"That's what I'm here for," Ali said, as she glanced at the beautiful cliffs surrounding her.

"I'm Ethan. I'd like to make the tour special for you, so I'll have to ask you some questions. Do you have an interest in past lives . . . and do you want me to show you the UFO ports?"

Ali extended her hand. "I'm Alicia." As he shook her hand, she noticed a snake tattoo going all the way up his arm. "All I can say is that I'm open. Is that good enough?"

"Right on. I'll just make sure I explain as we go along, and if you don't understand, please feel free to ask questions. I've been living in this area for about a thousand years, off and on, and I've been abducted quite a few times by the UFO's that frequent this area. You see that rock over there? It's called Bell Rock. It's actually an airport or a docking station for UFO's. You can sometimes see the space crafts hovering above it and then leaving on a horizontal path. Sometimes they're cloaked and appear like clouds." He motioned for Ali to follow him to the jeep, which was parked in the adjacent lot.

"Sometimes they look like clouds? A thousand years?" Ali whispered to Violetta. "Is this guy for real?"

"You'll have to decide for yourself what's *real*. That's why we're here," Vio answered.

The cloud comment seemed to be a real closer for Ali. Her feeling of skepticism and judgment gave her plenty of fuel to feel superior to the man who was about to take her life in his hands. Her assessment was that he was dressed like he was stuck in the '60s, he had strange tattoos, and he was acting as if he might have been smoking something, and not tobacco. Ethan interrupted her musings to tell her it was time to begin the tour.

"Before we go, take a minute to tune into how your body feels. Do you notice any unusual physical sensations since you arrived in Sedona? And your thoughts . . . are they any different from your normal thoughts?"

"Physical sensations? None really." Ali realized she was so busy thinking, she hadn't felt her body, and hardly noticed the beautiful landscape. She focused in on her body and did note some energy, especially in her palms and the soles of her feet. "Hmmm, the temperature is really nice. Energy . . . I do feel kind of tingly now that you mention it, and a little light-headed."

"So you can feel energy. That's a good start. I'll guide you as we go along."

"I'm game," Ali said, hoping that he didn't have the ability to read minds. She climbed into the jeep beside Ethan, and in the back seat, still invisible, were Vio and Layla.

"Ready to go? Fasten your seatbelt—the roads are rocky and I like to go fast. I'll describe some of the sites as we go."

She just tolerated the first ten minutes of the tour, as Ethan described the names of some of the local rock formations. "If you look to your right you'll see Coffee Pot Rock, and then a little further is Snoopy Rock . . ."

Ali questioned the purpose of naming rocks. It seemed like something you'd do for tourists. She thought it might be more fun to decide for herself what they looked like. Just as she had grown tired of identifying rocks, he pulled over and parked the jeep in a small lot filled with cars by a place he called "Airport Vortex." He asked Ali if she wouldn't mind hiking up a bit from the road. Ali noticed several groups of tourists making the climb, some already on top of a hill, so she concluded that it couldn't be too demanding.

"It's just a short walk up to a very beautiful old Indian power spot with an expansive view of the canyon." She reluctantly agreed, and Ethan jumped out of the jeep and circled the vehicle to open the door for Ali. He also opened the back door. Ali looked at him quizzically, but thought maybe he was letting out an insect or a lizard—hopefully not a rattlesnake or a scorpion. They began to walk up a winding path from the road and soon came to a high point from which they could see the entire valley. Along the way Ethan pointed out some markers made with rocks piled on top of each other and rock circles that he described as Indian prayer circles. Ali figured these were made by hippies and tourists in an attempt to get back to the earth, but nodded and acted appreciative. "And here is the Vortex. Can you feel it?"

That phrase was beginning to irritate Ali. "Can you feel it?" seemed to be the mantra of this area. All the people she passed along the way were saying exactly the same thing. "Sara, can you feel it? I can't, maybe a little over here. Didn't they say it was a little bit to the left?"

Ali couldn't feel anything, but luckily she wasn't interested in playing that game.

Vio decided that this might be the time for an intervention." Ali, have you had enough of your critical mind yet? Would you like to try another view?"

Ali could probably have gone through the entire visit in this mode and felt very satisfied with herself, but remembering that there might be another purpose to this visit, she agreed to allow Vio to change what she called her "frequency."

Ethan had walked away and was standing in the stone circle. Ali closed her eyes and opened them again. At first her vision was hazy. She rubbed her eyes with both fists, and then focused again. She looked at Ethan, and the first thing she saw was Layla jumping up on him and licking his face. He greeted Vio as if he knew her. Now she understood why he had so politely opened the back door of the jeep. It had been for them.

As she scanned the horizon, she saw eagles perched on the red outcroppings, hawks diving in arcs between the walls of the canyon, and hundreds of figures who looked like Indians, standing nobly along the rims on both sides. One of the Indians approached her. He was dressed in a feathered headdress, and he seemed ancient and timeless. Somehow she knew that these were not Indians, but their gods, the ones they called *Kachinas*. He nodded as though he understood her thoughts.

"Welcome to our sacred ground. We see that Ethan has brought you here. He told us that you almost missed the meeting. We are glad you were able to come."

Ali started shaking. The energy began moving rapidly through her body, and her heart felt very expansive, almost as though she were growing wings.

"This place they call Sedona is one of the most powerful locations sacred to us on this planet. In each of these sites there are guardians who have been here from the beginning to help you take good care of your home. Humans come here for many reasons. Even those who do not believe in us enjoy the energy and the healing that it provides. We need do nothing to assist in this. It simply brings people back to the original purpose. It's a purifying energy, it's a remembering energy, even if they see or hear nothing. You are fortunate that you can also see and hear us. We welcome your participation. There are many people who are alienated from their planet, so much so that they don't care if it continues at all. They are so removed from their original purpose, they live in pain while they are in paradise. You are standing, right now, in a place of pure beauty." Ali heard her inner voice saying, *I can feel it*, and then censored herself from thinking those words.

"Yes, you can feel it, we know. Bathe in it and realize that you are closer to your natural state now than ever before." Suddenly Ali felt her heart expanding and containing the entire canyon. She sensed that everything, every object, every person, every tree, was like a window into a limitless field of light—a doorway into infinity. And she was such a doorway as well. Then everything started to sparkle, and she saw the light no longer through the doorways, but sparkling in everything and everyone—even the tourist ladies who said, "Can you feel it? I can't feel it." It didn't matter anymore whether or not they could feel it. There was nothing to criticize, nothing to compare, nothing even to understand. There were no questions and no answers. "Ahhhh," she heard herself saying.

Vio, Layla and Ethan walked slowly over to Ali, and Layla licked her hand. They stood there together, for another moment, enjoying each other and all the magnificent beings, until the Indians began to fade, and the scene regained its normal appearance. "Wow!" was all Ali could say. She turned toward Ethan. "That was incredible. Who were those beings? Were they Indians, Kachinas, or Extra-Terrestrials?"

"Do you see how the questions only come back when the experience leaves?"

"Oh my, yes. But now that I'm back, I want to know."

"They exist on another dimension, and so do you, and so does everything. That's the only answer I can give. We humans are like radios. We have tuners that can tune to different stations. Vio is helping you to adjust your controls, but soon you will be able to adjust them at will. There are things to experience in all the dimensions. No one level of reality is better than another, although I suspect you prefer the one you just saw, in this stage of your growth."

"Don't you prefer that one too?"

"No, I love them all. Just because you prefer a hot fudge sundae to oatmeal, it doesn't mean you need to eat it for breakfast. You just enjoy the buffet, the spectrum of light and color that you can experience in the time when it is most appropriate."

"Who determines what and when is appropriate?"

"You do, but not the *you* that you think you are."

"What?"

"Vio will help you with that later. For now, I think you might want to have some time to take in what you have experienced today. I'll return you in the jeep to the starting point and wish you well."

And this he did, and all was well, as he wished.

Ali found herself back in her loft on Fifth Avenue, resting on her couch, still basking in the light she had just experienced on her visit to Sedona. She reflected that she had never felt more complete, and she knew that what she was feeling encompassed much more than the fulfillment of any human desire—even a loft in Chelsea.

9

Cancer Group

Just as Ali was getting ready to make the drive again to the cottage, she heard a scratching sound coming from the hallway. She walked to the door and looked through the small security peephole, but saw nothing, until she looked down and into the soulful eyes of Layla, the inter-dimensional dog. She opened the door and welcomed Layla, (who was in physical form this morning,) and Violetta, (who had forsaken physical form, and appeared to Ali as a translucent being).

"May we come in?" Vio requested politely, as if Ali would ever consider refusing her entry.

"Of course, welcome."

Layla came in through the doorway, Vio came in literally through the door.

"Welcome. Please have a seat; I'll put on the kettle." Vio sat down at the small, round kitchen table, and watched Ali as she prepared her drink—with the beautiful chrome and copper espresso machine that had appeared on the counter that morning. In Vio's house the coffee just materialized, but in

Ali's loft she still needed to do the work. As she pressed the coffee grounds carefully into the filter, she remembered Ethan's teaching about how there are great joys to be experienced in the physical dimension. Preparing espresso, she thought, was surely one of them.

Ali completed her preparations, and silently placed the two cups on the table. She hesitated, at first, and then started to speak. "Vio, I had some very strange experiences last night when I returned from Sedona, and I'm not sure I want another adventure like that today. I don't know if I could handle the intensity."

"It was a very powerful day for you, dear. Why don't you tell me what's been happening?"

"Well, it's weird, and you may think I'm nuts, but as I was nodding off in front of the television, I had an energetic sensation that felt like an MRI machine was moving energy through my body. I was instructed to relax and let it work for me. It focused primarily around my head and neck, and I was told that there was a misalignment of energy, and that 'they' were correcting it. The 'treatment' continued for a few minutes longer, until I decided to go to my bed and let it continue there—but it stopped. Did I make a mistake by interrupting the process? Also, can you explain what happened, and who 'they' are?"

"First of all, Ali, you can't make a mistake. I know it's hard for you to believe that, but some day you'll know for certain. In response to your second question, you had a powerful dose of light yesterday, more than your body was used to. What you experienced last night was real—although the image of the MRI was yours. It was necessary that some adjustments be made to your body so that it could incorporate yesterday's experience. There was some realignment and some recalibration.

"You asked who 'they' are. They are part of a team of helpers who work with you—and many others—whenever necessary. This happens more often than you think, but it's usually done during deep sleep. I don't want you to get too involved in the 'who' and 'how' aspects. Just know you're being taken care of."

Ali took a deep breath and exhaled. "This is a lot to take in. I don't know if I'm ready for any more right now, Vio."

"I'm glad you're checking in with yourself, and I am aware of your situation. Today I'll take you on a trip where you'll learn more by observation than by experiencing energetically; and this will give your body some additional time to adjust. How does that feel?"

"It feels appropriate on many levels." She answered.

Vio stepped behind Ali—who was still seated at the table—and pressed her palms downward on Ali's shoulders. "Okay, that's better. You were rising a bit from the chair. I want you to learn to remain grounded on this plane as you travel in the other dimensions."

"I didn't feel like I was rising. My behind was on the chair."

"Yes, the physical body stayed on the chair, but the *etheric body* was starting to rise, and not in a controlled way."

"I'll take your word for it. Your hands certainly feel good on my shoulders. I'm so glad you're here to help me with these details."

"The teachings couldn't happen without a guide. It would be irresponsible of us."

"Does that ever happen?" Ali asked.

"Yes, sometimes in places where the energy is very strong, or in times of great stress, people go through initiations or openings, but are sometimes unable to understand what's happening to them. They might think they're having a nervous breakdown or a heart attack, and often seek medical attention. Of course there are very few physicians who are familiar with these types of symptoms, so they are often misdiagnosed.

"I guess I'm really lucky to have you, Vio."

"You are fortunate to have been chosen, but you've been asking for these teachings for quite a long time. It was no accident that we met in this time and space.

"Now, let's get back to the present. Do you have any questions about anything we've discussed thus far today?"

"Yes, actually I do. The experiences with the MRI, and the healing you offered me this morning bring up some questions about healing in general."

Vio gave Ali her total attention, sensing that this was a difficult subject for her.

"I feel very awkward saying this—it's not a very popular position to take—but I guess I could describe myself as a 'disillusioned healer.' I studied so many healing techniques over the years, (physical, psychological and even spiritual methods), and I enthusiastically taught them to others. But based on experience and intuition, Vio, I'm not sure that we, as limited human beings, even have the ability to influence whether someone lives or dies. I guess I'd like to think there's a higher power at work in making those decisions. I've also been in the presence of very powerful healers who seemed to effect miraculous cures, but often the illnesses reappeared at a later time. And people around these healers, including myself, wanted so much for it to be true that we would ignore the facts, even when they were staring us in the face.

"Now this issue is activated for me because a friend of mine has been diagnosed with breast cancer. She knows my past experience as a healer and is asking for my help. Honestly, Vio, I don't know what healing is or how to access it anymore. The whole idea of even considering healing someone else makes my brain short-circuit. I feel reluctant to even think in those terms anymore. In fact, I don't even think I could if I wanted to."

"So this healing you received last night and the experience of my hands on your shoulder must have contradicted your belief that healing is unavailable. Is that correct?"

"Yes, exactly."

"Ali, before we go any further, I'd like you to take a look at why you're attached to either belief."

Ali paused for a moment, when all of a sudden tears welled up in her eyes and her lips began to tremble. The words poured out as if they'd been dammed up for years. "Oh God, it makes me feel like maybe there was more I could have done for my parents. I felt it was God's will that they passed, but now that I'm experiencing miraculous healing in your presence, I'm thinking that maybe there was something else I could have done!"

Vio took Ali's hands in hers and looked lovingly into her eyes. "Oh dear, what a huge can of worms we've opened. It's very good that all of this is coming out now, and I promise that today's visit will help you to see beyond the paradox of whether or not *we* can heal.

"We're staying here, in New York, for this one. There's a group called 'Breast Cancer Sisters' at the Medical Center right around the corner. I'd like you to sit in on their meeting."

Ali walked over to the coat rack, grabbed her jacket and purse, and stood by the door, awaiting Vio's next move. "Are we walking or flying this time?"

"I think walking is appropriate today. It's a little chilly out, and I think you'd look conspicuous if you didn't have a little color in your cheeks when you arrive."

The trio entered the lobby of the Cancer Center, although Ali was the only visible one among them. Vio directed her to the door of the conference room where the cancer support group was just about to begin.

Ali was wondering how she was going to talk herself into the group, when a woman in a nurse's uniform welcomed her. "I'm Sandy Berkeley, the Group Facilitator . . . and you must be Alicia." Ali nodded, discreetly checking her jacket to see if she was wearing a name tag. She wasn't. "Welcome. I was told to expect you. Please come and join our circle." Ali wondered what Vio had told Sandy to merit such a welcome.

As Sandy added an extra chair for her, Ali recognized her friend Janet, sitting directly across the circle. *Why am I surprised?* She muttered to herself.

Sandy opened the meeting and suggested they go around clock-wise and introduce themselves. Ali shifted uncomfortably in her seat. *Vio didn't tell me my cover story. What am I supposed to say?* But her thoughts were interrupted by Sandy, who introduced Ali to the group as a visiting psychologist who was working primarily with breast cancer patients. *That works*, Ali thought. *Maybe some day I'll learn to trust Violetta.*

Following the initial introductions, the discussion became more personal, as the women shared the stories of their diagnoses, treatments, and how they were coping with the changes in their lives. Ali listened intently, jotting down her impressions in her notebook. She used fictitious names to protect the privacy of the patients. Ali's notebook looked like this:

1. Red Haired Woman – Wears red wig, mastectomy, chemotherapy, following allopathic medical treatment w/out question. Name tag on blouse underneath jacket says "Dr. . . . at another hospital. Didn't tell group she's an M.D.

2. Warrior Woman - bald, wearing head scarf, chemo. Pride in baldness, doesn't like wigs not "real self." Macrobiotic diet, misses chocolate. Facing cancer like warrior [her words]. Stage two. She's my friend.

3. Zen Meditator - Her *Roshi* recently died of cancer. Feels special since she has same illness, maybe sign of spiritual advancement. Using meditation for healing. Conflicted about teacher's death and effectiveness of meditation. Using allopathic medicine as backup. Says it will be okay if she dies because spirit will live on. Says she's unattached. I'd be confused too.

4. Mother of Five - Terrified children will lose their mother. Will go to extremes, even bone marrow transplant. Researched alternative methods in Mexico if insurance doesn't cover treatment. Lost mother to breast cancer at thirteen and suffered through adolescence without her. Would do anything to avoid this for her children. I feel sad for her.

5. Health Freak - Has devoted her life to health to avoid the "Big C." Organic vegetarian diet, avoided pollutants, never used carcinogenic products i.e. bug sprays, make-up or commercial detergents, plastic. Recently learned childhood home was built on chromium landfill. Very angry, pursuing class action lawsuit. Ironic.

6. Angelic Woman - Wearing ethereal clothing. Artist, paints angels. Not grounded. How does she live in New York? Seems detached from body. Doesn't care if she lives or dies. Came to group for her mother. Says she's at peace with diagnosis.

7. Fashion Model – Looks like model. Seems superficial. double mastectomy and chemo, breast reconstruction. Trying to hide condition. Beautiful long wig, penciled eyebrows, false eyelashes. Red cocktail dress. Maybe I'm too judgmental!

8. Guilty Mother - Gay son died of AIDS. Beats herself up, thinks cancer is payback. Said if she dies she will be free of the guilt.

9. Miraculous Cure Woman – Diagnosed w/fourth stage cancer and attended healing seminar at holistic/spiritual clinic. Shortly after seminar, cancer disappeared overnight. Came to group to offer inspiration. I'm impressed! Tells about the diet she followed and seminar. Someone asks if anyone else was healed. She didn't think so. Too bad they asked. I like her a lot.

10. Remission Woman – Was in remission for ten years, cancer metastasized in her bones. Grateful for the ten years because able to raise children. Had near death experience years ago. Because of that, she's not afraid to die. Inspiring!

Just as Ali completed her writing, Sandy suggested they take a short break and return in fifteen minutes. About half the women gathered in groups to continue their conversations, a few went to the tables along the side of the room to look at the literature, and others left the meeting room in search of the restroom. Ali walked out into the lobby so that she could be alone with Violetta.

"So who is going to survive, Vio?"

"I was just going to ask you the same question. Who do you think?"

Ali re-read her notes and then came up with her response. "I think the one with the overnight remission, the one with the children, maybe the physician, and I hope the warrior." She then started to second-guess her response. The more she thought about it, the more her brain seemed to short-circuit—a new sensation for her since she had met Vio. She had a feeling that thinking just might not provide the answers she was seeking.

"Are you ready for the next phase of this learning?" Vio asked.

"I can't wait. Let's do it." Ali returned to her seat in the circle, just in time to see an amazing show.

She felt as though Vio had turned up the thermostat, and the energy in the room took on a golden glow. At first the room was awash with light, but then, as Ali's eyes became more accustomed to the new atmosphere, she was able to see the ten women in the circle; but now there were more than ten women, there were at least twenty—counting the angels, (or whatever they were). There was one hovering around each woman, and one around the nurse leading the group, and others standing toward the back of the room, observing, almost as if they were being instructed.

Ali noticed Layla, in spirit form, moving about the room. The angelic woman was the first to notice her, as she put her arm down and petted Layla on her head and back. Layla wagged her tail. The angelic woman's angel looked a lot like she did. They were both filled with light. Ali was able to intuit the message of the angel. She was telling the woman that she was being given a choice to live or die, and either one would be acceptable. The woman was favoring the choice to leave her body at this point, but was being told that this could change if she were able to experience the love available to her on the earth plane. The angel was working with her on this. Ali was cheering for her to stay but felt intuitively that it would be okay either way.

Looking around the circle, Ali saw that many of the women, on some level, were aware of the angelic assistance they were receiving—and she could also tell that the assistance was not about "healing" per se, it was about pure love.

While she was observing the angelic activity, Ali understood that although these women had gathered here to increase their chances of survival, at the same time—whether known or unknown to their conscious minds—their souls were benefiting as well, and they were immortal.

Vio asked Ali to show her the one who was most receptive to the energy and assistance of her guide, and which one was the least receptive. Ali, of course, had her preconceived ideas. She thought perhaps the Zen Meditator or the Angelic Woman were the most receptive, and the Fashion Model was the least receptive. Her eyes told her otherwise. The Zen Meditator was radiating light, but the light was contained in a bubble. She almost resembled a light bulb with a glass completely circling her body. Outside of the bulb was a field of much brighter light.

Vio explained to Ali, telepathically, what her eyes were showing her. "Ali, what you're seeing is accurate. The concepts of the Zen Meditator are actually interfering with her ability to receive the light and knowledge that is being offered to her."

Ali was amazed. She had been very impressed with this woman's credentials and even her acceptance of a kind of spiritual martyrdom.

Vio continued, "There is a subtle but very powerful difference between true spiritual experience and the concept of what might be called 'spiritual specialness.' This is the biggest trap for people on the spiritual path. The ego can be very insidious in intelligent people, because they are often very good at figuring out how to be spiritual. But 'figuring out' is a mental activity and really bears no relationship whatsoever to true spiritual realization.

Ali saw herself in this description and asked, silently, "How can I recognize the difference?"

"In a true experience of 'Self' connected with all beings, what would 'specialness' mean?"

Ali pondered this question and realized that there could never be specialness in the experience of Oneness. It was impossible to imagine. No matter how many years she meditated, or what robes or credentials she earned, or classes she taught. . . it was all irrelevant in the light of Truth. She saw how even the concept of healing paled when viewed from this perspective.

Ali started thinking back over her previous spiritual experiences when Vio interrupted her reverie with the question, "And how about the Warrior? What do you see happening with her?"

"As you know, Vio, the Warrior is my friend Janet. I see energy projected from her heart and from her solar plexus. It's powerful. I could even feel that before I shifted into this plane. But the odd thing is that the power she is projecting is not connected to the power that is being showered on her by her guide. It's like she's a radio operating on batteries, even though it's plugged into the wall. She doesn't need to run on batteries, they're only the backup. She could just let the energy coming from the source move her. Her misunderstanding is that she thinks *she* has to do it."

"Yes, Ali. She might be successful in spurts, but this kind of action will eventually wear her down. Maybe then she'll become receptive to the energy around her."

Ali thought for a moment and then shared with Vio, "Janet had expressed to me a lot of anxiety about the concept 'you create your own reality.' At first she was very inspired by the idea, and was using it to make things happen for herself. She was able to manifest a new job and was working on creating a boyfriend when she received the cancer diagnosis. Now she's feeling very guilty and confused because she believes that since she was able to manifest the job she imagined, she should also be able to make the cancer go away. She also wonders why she *created* the disease in the first place."

Vio sighed and said, "Oh, my dear, if you only knew how many people suffer so much under that delusion. It's really a disservice to so many to give them the illusion that they can do anything. Now, it is true in one way, if you use the word 'You' to refer to your 'True Self,' the aspect of you that is connected with all other Selves and is the creative energy of the Universe. Only in that context is the statement true, and it is my hope that people will come to see that reality sooner than later.

"And now, Ali, one more question before the meeting ends. Who is the one most receptive to her guides?"

Ali's glance went from one to another with no immediate results. She then decided to soften her gaze and just allow the light to permeate her eyes to see which one shined the brightest. "Oh, it couldn't be, could it?" She was afraid to respond, thinking she would be wrong. "Is it the Fashion Model?" Ali asked.

"Yes. You're correct. I'm glad you chose to trust what you experienced over your intellectual judgments."

"But how could it be? She has no concept of anything beyond her body? She's not spiritual. She probably has never meditated a day in her life. All she thinks about is her body, and she's in denial about her disease."

"Yes, all of that is true, and all of that is irrelevant, totally irrelevant. And Ali, there is no way to know why, no way at all. This woman is surrounded by light, inside and out—and look, Layla is sitting in her lap. You see, Ali, she is loved, and she knows it—regardless of her limited beliefs. Isn't that miraculous? And she is operating on the true source of energy, not the batteries. She is totally innocent of what is happening."

Ali shook her head and said, "Another concept bites the dust. I think the best thing to do is to lose *all* my concepts."

"And where have you heard that before?" Vio asked.

"Probably from every spiritual teaching I've ever read, but I thought they just wanted to brainwash me with their own concepts. Now I see the truth in the statement that we really don't know anything, and that our concepts and judgments only interfere with seeing reality."

"Now, Ali, before the group breaks up and we have to leave, take another look from behind your eyes, through what I sometimes call 'God's eyes,' and describe what you see."

Ali shifted to a soft focus, allowing her eyes to passively take in what was happening in the meeting room. "I see ten unique women, each struggling within her limited belief system, and yet they are all connected in a web of light coming from their hearts and third eyes in a beautiful intertwining pattern. And they are all bathed in golden light from the beautiful beings flying around and between them. Vio, you did it again!"

Ali thanked the leader of the group and all the members for allowing her to observe. She wished she could tell them what she saw. She hoped that in the future there might be some way she could do that. But regardless, she knew they were all blessed beyond their wildest dreams.

As she was leaving the meeting room, Ali saw Janet speaking with the nurse. She caught herself hoping that Janet wouldn't notice her, but realized that would be inappropriate, if not outright rude. She hoped Vio could help her out of this awkward situation.

"Vio, Janet is over there and will probably approach me before I get out of the door. I'm feeling at a loss here. Now that I've seen what she's doing with her energy, how can I still offer my support? And I know she'll be expecting some healing energy or advice from me."

Vio responded, "I see how you'd feel that way. Whenever a new understanding is reached, there will be some changes in the way you relate to your world and the people in it. This is a situation that we all encounter as we evolve. Your question is valid. How can you relate to Janet with the new insights you have into healing, and the way she's using her energy? What if I were to say that your insights into her particular situation are irrelevant, totally irrelevant?"

"I'd ask then why I was shown these visions today."

"You were shown the truth of the situation to impress you with how inadequate your thinking is about healing, as well as life and death. Now that you realize that your concepts are at odds with what is in front of you, are you willing to let them go—even the concepts about angels and energy sources?"

"Are you asking me to forget what I just witnessed?"

"Not to forget, but know that when you see Janet, you will not be using any of that information. Your challenge is to be present for her without any agendas, any concepts, and any idea of who you are or who she is. What I am asking you to do is to try not to see yourself as a 'healer' and Janet as a 'patient.' Just be present. That's all."

"Right now?"

"She seems to be approaching you. I'm here, and I'll assist you. Just drop everything and be present, and you'll see what happens."

Janet turned from the group that had gathered around the nurse, and caught Ali's eye. Ali shook her wrists to clear her personal energy, and began walking toward Janet. In the moment they met, before they could say a word, Ali felt an opening in her crown center at the top of her head, and an influx of energy that moved down into the center of her chest. The feeling was so full she felt her heart was overflowing with golden light. In the next moment the energy began to move from her heart into her arms and hands. She effortlessly raised her arms as Janet moved toward her to receive the embrace. She could feel Janet relax as the energy from her heart entered Janet's heart, and her hands on Janet's back, seemed to soothe her and bless her. The energy continued to flow between them until Ali felt it was time to step back. She took Janet's hands in hers and looked into her eyes. She could feel that Janet's energy had shifted, and that her friend was finally connected with her True Self.

"Ali, that was incredible. I just knew you had something for me today. I felt it when I saw you in the circle. I feel renewed." Janet was radiant.

Ali knew that what had just transpired had nothing to do with "Ali the healer." She felt herself bowing and saying the simple words, "Janet, it was wonderful seeing you today." Janet bowed in return, and walked slowly through the lobby and out the door.

Ali had an idea about what had just transpired, but it raised a few questions as well. "Vio, that wasn't me. I had no idea what was going to happen. And it looks like she 'got it.' She seemed to be connected to her True Being—but oddly enough, I couldn't tell her, I couldn't teach her. I knew it would have broken the connection."

"Yes, I'm glad you saw that. She didn't need any words, and they weren't given to you to say. You followed the energy as it was given to you, and I'm very pleased that you were able to set your ideas aside. You see, Ali, the only thing that is important for you to learn and for you to share is the beauty of the One Being. Everything was contained in that embrace—everything that is known and unknown, everything that is you, and everything that is Janet. There is nothing else to know and nothing else to do."

"But will she continue to be as connected to her True Self as she is now?"

"We don't know that, do we, Ali? And is she less her True Self if she doesn't know it?"

"Of course not. That would be impossible."

"That's correct, Ali."

"Well, that's so much easier, Vio." Ali felt the energy begin to move through her body. She began to recognize that whenever she felt a chill, it meant that a Truth had been spoken.

Ali sensed it was time to leave, and although her body had received the truth of today's lesson, her mind was still unresolved. She entered the front door with Vio and Layla beside her, and exited alone.

10

Human Suffering

Ali rolled over in bed, and then attuned her ears to a din that seemed to be coming at her in stereo. The feeling of expansiveness that loft living provided had its downside—as her bedroom shared two common walls with her neighbors. She glanced at the alarm. It was six forty-five a.m., and the natives were already restless.

Some noises are more easily tuned out than others. TV, radio, garbage trucks in the early morning, the beeping of horns on a busy New York through street were all easy to ignore, but the sounds of anger caught and held her attention. She learned, that morning, that the apartment directly adjacent to hers on the north side had a teenaged daughter and two very dismayed parents. Simultaneously she "met" the neighbor on the south side, who was having a terrible fight with his partner—and all so early in the morning.

The first voice Ali heard was a strong, controlled male voice. "You have obligations, as a member of this family, and based upon your low grades and your inability to come home before your curfew, you have shown yourself undeserving of what you call your freedom."

The response came from a shrill and teary adolescent female voice. "I don't care what you think! You're old! You don't understand about popularity. I *can't* leave a party early because my parents say so. They'll all be laughing at me. I'm sixteen years old. I know what I'm doing. You can trust me! I'm fed up with being treated like a child!"

The third voice was that of the mother. "I remember what it's like to be in high school, and I know that you want to fit in . . . but your father and I have certain rules, and you will find out, later in life, that it's necessary that you learn them now so you will be successful later. Do you understand where we're coming from? I had a very uncaring mother, and I swore, when I had a child of my own, that I would honor her feelings and love her. I love you very much; show me you love me by listening to us and following the rules we set out for you."

"I don't care where you're coming from! I'm not living my life to make you comfortable. I'm suffocating in this little apartment. I want out. I want to get out of here and find out who I am. I don't want to be the little girl that you dress up and show off to people. I don't care about my grades, or going to college, or marrying well. That's all for you. I tried to fit the pattern, and now I'm waking up to the truth. Those things are bullshit. I look in the mirror and see a fake girl smiling back. Her face is cracking, the mirror is cracking. It's all a sham. None of this is true. I want out! I want out now!"

Her father's voice responded, with added volume, "You're sixteen, for God's sake! What do you mean, 'Trust me!' You're a child and you still need us. You'll follow our rules, or you'll be sorry."

"I don't care what you say. I'll stay out all night if I want to. And what are you going to do about it, hit me? I'll report you and they'll take me away from you."

There was silence in apartment 5A, and Ali, sitting up in bed, shifted her attention to the voices of Apartment 5C coming through the opposite wall of her apartment. She wondered if there was something in the water.

A woman's voice was the first one she heard. "I've wasted the best years of my life on you. You're so controlling. I can't be myself with you. You embarrassed me last night at the dinner party."

"I embarrassed *you*? Are you kidding me?"

"You don't tell me how to dress when we're dining with your boss. I think I looked really 'hot.' I think he thought so too. I know what enough cleavage is; believe me, it's what attracted you in the first place. And incidentally, I know how much I can drink and still be in control."

"Honey, calm down. You know I love you."

"You didn't act like that last night. You were just trying to control me. You treated me like a child, just like you're doing now."

You know it's important for me to make a good impression with the boss. I have to sell out all the time to get ahead. Why won't you help me by not sabotaging me? Baby, you know I need you, and you need me. We love each other—"

"I'm not so sure I love you. I'll bet there's someone out there who will love me the way I am, and won't tell me to change. I'm thinking I want to go out there and find him."

"I do love you the way you are, but relationships are never easy. We just need to make compromises sometimes. If it's freedom you want, we could go look for a car for you today. . . think about it. Baby, come back to bed. Don't turn your back on me."

Ali's head was spinning. Her degree in psychology should offer some insight into what might help these people, but at seven a.m. her analytical mind was feeling very fuzzy. She found it ironic, because relationships had been her specialty before she retired. "I wonder what Vio would do?" she said aloud.

Vio and Layla appeared, as if they had been summoned. "Good morning, Ali. So how do you like loft living so far?" Vio took a seat at the table and invited Ali to take the seat opposite her. Layla lay on the floor between them.

"Well, it has its benefits and drawbacks. Both my neighbors are embroiled in huge fights. On one side is a teenager fighting with her parents, and on the other is a quarreling couple. I'm living in the middle of chaos. I wish you could have heard what I heard this morning so that you could you help me to understand them better."

"That's easy to do. Let's re-run what I've missed. Just hold on, it will only take a minute." Ali held tightly to her chair as everything around her, with the exception of Vio, Layla, and the kitchen table, went into fast rewind mode before her eyes. Then Vio stopped the action and Ali saw herself lying in her bed, with the alarm clock showing the time as six forty-five. When they had listened to the fifteen-minute dialogue, including Ali asking for help from Vio, they returned to "real time." Violetta poured herself a cup of tea from a pot, which had just appeared on the table. Ali lifted her coffee cup to her lips.

"So, Ali, let's see what you've 'learned' this morning."

At first, Ali was surprised at the remark, but was happy to offer her insights. "I can tell that the father is the disciplinarian. He is laying out boundaries for his daughter because he believes that if she has the proper boundaries in childhood, she'll be able to continue the discipline in her life. The mother is trying to be compassionate. It's almost like they're playing good cop/bad cop—but unintentionally. She wants the daughter to be able to express her emotions and to feel heard. I don't think the daughter sees it that way."

"And the daughter, what's going on with her?"

"The daughter is feeling caged in by the father's discipline and enmeshed by the mother's needs. Just like any teenager, she's moved by her hormones, and peer pressure. She's in a stage of life where she is feeling compelled to individuate. Judging by the father's philosophy of child training and the mother's overindulgence, it may be that the child never made the first move toward independence at two years old, and so now she's trying to do it, but even more forcefully. That's a simple assessment based upon my analysis of psychological tasks." Realizing that she hadn't taken a breath during her presentation, Ali sat back in her chair. "What do you think of that?"

"Well Ali, that was quite a thorough analysis. Let's move on to Apartment 5C."

Ali was disappointed that Vio didn't offer any feedback on her perceptions, but hoped she would later on. "I'm assuming, based on the conversation, that the woman is attractive and probably younger than the man. I can't tell if they're married or not."

"How do you analyze the relationship then?"

"I'd say the male has taken on society's values for what makes him a man. That would include success in his job, an expensive home, and a sexy partner waiting for him when he comes home from work. I would guess that appearance is a major concern for him.

"The woman, judging by her voice and vocabulary, comes from a lower social level than he does, and probably considers herself fortunate to live with a man of means, in such an upscale district. When faced with a decision to come or go, she is easily swayed by his materialistic offers and feels safe with him. The security of a man who says he loves her and supports her seems more important than any other considerations, and that's why she's still there. I think her turning away from him is part of a game she plays. I won't be surprised if I see a new car in the garage tomorrow.

"From what I know about relationships—which might have a cynical note to it since I'm alone—is that what most people call 'love' is more about need. The man needs feminine energy (anima), and the woman needs masculine energy (animus), in order to feel complete—it's just basic Jungian psychology. And both are willing to put up with a certain amount of compromise in order to have that balance. The man is both controlling and jealous. He knows how the woman was when he met her and has an underlying fear that she will leave him. He has abandonment issues for sure. In fact, she holds that up to him in order to prevail in their fights—which I suspect are frequent. She is expressing the need for freedom, which makes sense since he does want to limit her freedom. He also wants to determine how she should look in order to impress others. This is very similar to the experience of the daughter in 5A.

"So, Vio, now what do you have to tell me, or show me?"

"I believe that what you've observed could be expressed in one sentence. People seek freedom and love, but they search for it in all the wrong places."

"You mean like in Rumi's poem about the flute?"

"Good, I'm glad you found the poem. Yes. When one is truly aware of his or her True Self, is there any question about freedom? It's no coincidence that there are prisoners who have achieved enlightenment while incarcerated (Nelson Mandela and Anwar Sadat in prison, and Jack Schwartz in a concentration camp). These are extreme examples, but they prove the point that freedom, although desired on the material plane by all humans, is truly, on another dimension, available all the time.

"The other demonstration we saw here is the desire to be validated. This is also a desire for something which is already available, as you know, on the plane of pure existence. You call it 'Love' with a capital 'L'. You learned about that in Switzerland, didn't you?"

"So, Vio, you're saying that all their unhappiness is caused by their belief that they're lacking something that they really already have. How absurd and sadly funny it all is."

Ali sat back and reflected on what had just been said. *If it were simply that all human pain comes from an illusion about who we think we are, why did I have to do all that analysis? Why did I spend all those years studying psychology? Analyzing makes me feel smart, but does it really benefit the client in the end? How can I really help anyone?"*

Vio gazed directly into her eyes, with a look so powerful it sent a chill through Ali's body. "Are you ready to stop yet?"

"Stop what?"

"Ali, I want you to take a look at this scene from an energetic point of view."

"Oh, you mean the daughter taking energy from the parents, and the lover stealing energy from her partner?"

"No," she said sternly. Ali wondered if Vio wasn't getting fed up with her. "My dear soul, what is happening to your energy?"

"You mean right now?"

"Well, let's make it simple. You were lying in bed this morning, and you heard the family on your right and the couple on your left. I'll make a little drawing here for you, and you tell me if that is what your energy felt like?" Vio made a simple drawing, on a paper napkin, that looked to Ali almost like a daddy long legs.

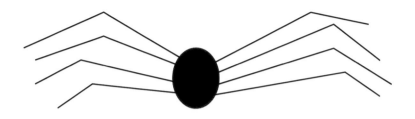

"I don't get it. My energy is like a spider?"

"That's how it looks to me. Do you see the central body? That represents your body, which is a receiver of energy, right? And the legs are strands of attention that you sent out in both directions. You're sitting in your room, but your attention, or your energy, is really in apartments 5A and 5C. What has happened to 5B?"

"Well, here in 5B I'm thinking about 5A and 5C, so I'm not totally gone."

"That's correct. So the body is a bunch of thoughts, which may or may not be correct. You really don't have all the facts, do you? This is all conjecture and theory that you've learned in school or have observed in others, or how you would feel in that same situation. It has very little relationship to what is really happening to you in the moment. Where are *you*, Ali?"

"I'm a bunch of thoughts, I guess, as you described."

"And is that *who* you are? Who else are you?"

"Well, if I take back the legs, or the strands, I'm just being myself."

"Yes, and if the yelling is happening on all sides of you, how does the *whole you* experience the situation?"

"Well, my first impression is that it would just be sound. But what if there really was a need for intervention?"

"Ali, this is something you will have to experience to understand, but if you are centered in yourself, that means you are connected with all aspects of yourself, in all the dimensions. And you needn't be consciously aware of it—it just happens when your attention is focused within your own being. Then, when you are being asked to do an action in the world, it will come through you automatically, without analysis and without effort."

Just as Ali was about to argue her point, the light fixture above the table where they sat, broke loose from the ceiling and fell onto the table top. In that split second, before it hit the table, Ali moved back, out of the way of the falling lamp. Ali realized she was totally calm as the lamp fell. It was only afterwards that her body reacted to the danger.

"How did you know to move out of the way, Ali? Did you figure anything out first?"

"No, I guess I just did it."

As Vio sent the light fixture back to its original position, she smiled at Ali. "I know it's a lot to ask at this time—but the more you trust the Universe, the more situations like this will happen, and it will reinforce the fact that you will know what you need to know, and you will do what you need to do. So you see, Ali, there is nothing to be done by *you* in either of these situations. Let me ask you something that will probably throw your ego off its game. What is the value of analysis in this situation? Think about it before you answer."

"Well, Vio, to be totally honest, fighting scares me, and figuring it out makes me feel safer. I guess it's the way I deal with fear in general, by figuring it out. But, as you pointed out, my energy is scattered when I'm analyzing, so I'm really not any safer at all, am I?"

"That's a very good understanding you have just demonstrated. Yes, you scatter your energy because you are afraid, and you think it will help you. That's essentially why it's so hard to stay centered, and so ironic; because, as you just experienced, the safety is already there when you're centered. To put it even more accurately, Ali, there isn't even an issue of safety when you trust."

Ali took a deep breath, straightening her back in her chair. A chill went through her body as her energy found its correct pathway. As Ali and Vio sat together in silence, the two neighbors, as if on cue, started yelling again. Ali kept her center, and the fighting words began to sound more like barking dogs or singing birds. When she wasn't focusing on the content, it was just sound, it was life, it was people just doing their thing. There was no impulse to avoid or hide—and, interestingly enough, the sounds soon faded into the background noises of the trucks, the honking horns and the people on the street. Ali sat in total peace. "Vio, would you like another cup of tea?" she asked.

They sat for a moment, delighting in each other's presence. And then, as Ali cleared the table and moved the dishes to the sink, she turned back to ask another question, but Vio and Layla were gone. Her questions would have to wait until tomorrow.

11
A New View

Although Ali now had the route to Blue Swan Lake essentially on automatic pilot, she had an intuition that she wouldn't be seeing much of Violetta's house in the future. Her premonition was justified when she again heard the scratching at her loft door, bright and early. Vio, having been born in a gentler time, still knocked—even though she could appear at will anywhere she wished. Ali appreciated this touch of civility, even though she knew that all bets were off as soon as she agreed to the next journey. This morning Ali had a few questions, one of which was related to this very issue.

"Good morning, Ali. Yesterday, although our visit was short, you were challenged to drop your analytical approach to reality. That involved quite a shift for you. Some days will be like that. Do you have any unfinished business or questions regarding yesterday's experience, or Monday's perhaps?"

"Yes. But first of all, I wonder if I will ever be meeting you at the lake house anymore, and why you have started to come here."

"That's simple. You have only to remember the state of mind you were in on the first two visits to Blue Swan Lake. If you recall, the first day you were almost scared off by my neighbor, Eddie, with his rifle; and the second day you were afraid of a cup of espresso put on the table according to your own wishes. It was only on the third day that you took a sip—which was only the beginning of your acceptance of alternative realities. I had to take you slowly, as slowly as you indicated to me. I know it's probably even difficult for you to remember now how you felt at the beginning of our collaboration."

"It really feels like another lifetime," Ali answered.

"That description is accurate. You have come a long way. But, you see, I still must base my teachings on what you can accept—on a conscious and unconscious level. As you have noticed, the lessons have been increasing in intensity in accordance with your ability to expand your beliefs."

"Thank you. That makes total sense. My second question is about the model in the cancer group on Monday, the one who was the most receptive to the energy. If innocence works the best, how can one be receptive when one is not so innocent?"

"I believe there is another question behind that one. Correct me if I'm wrong, but are you asking if there is anything you can *do* to be enlightened?"

"Yes, I'm ashamed to say it, and I know what your answer will be."

"And what will my answer be?" Vio asked.

"That *doing* is already antithetical to enlightenment. That seems to be what I've been seeing so far."

"Ali, let's go look together at the experiences you've had over the last week. Under what circumstances were you able to see what was true—behind the façade of thought and imagination?"

"When I stopped thinking and judging. But how can I stop thinking without thinking?"

"I suggest that you just continue the course with me. After a while, moving between dimensions—as you were shown in the tarot card of the Seven of Swords—will become more like second nature to you.

"But, Ali, I also want to warn you not to create a technique out of this. You see, the way I am working with you is based upon *your* present belief system and *your* level of understanding in this moment in time. Other people, at different stages of growth, with different reference points, will respond better to other methods."

"Vio, you're reading my mind again. Whenever I have some kind of new understanding, I want to conceptualize it and then teach it to others. But when I tried in the past, it never seemed to work."

"That's right, Ali. I'm asking you to stop the habit of trying to pin down the Truth. The only person who can benefit from these experiences and these teachings is you. Any thoughts you have about how you want to influence someone else are just thoughts, and they take your focus away from knowing who you are."

"It's hard for me to notice when I'm doing that."

"Okay, I'll help you to recognize when it's happening. Just imagine, for a moment, a realization you've had recently, and then remember what it was like in your body when the first thoughts came in."

"Yes, Vio, I can bring back the experience I had in Switzerland. The first thoughts were: 'How can I stay in this feeling of Love?' or 'How can I share this understanding?' or 'What does this experience mean?' And the questions felt constricting, like putting on tight shoes. My energy seemed to move from my heart to my head, and the realization that I was trying to pass on or save had already become rigid, and I'd already turned it into a concept or a belief."

"I'm glad, Ali, that you can feel the difference in your body. You see 'no thinking' is the best approach. One day you will really understand that this is true and not just a spiritual platitude."

"Okay, Vio, but I still have some unanswered questions about the cancer group. Is it okay for me to ask?"

"Of course, Ali. Let's get all your questions out in the open."

"I saw all those women in the circle, and I saw how some were more receptive to the angels than others; but you didn't answer my question of who will get healed."

"Ah, you are now asking something beyond the realm of even my understanding. I know that my job, and the job of those guides you saw around those women, is only to help them to bathe in their own beingness. Whether their bodies continue in this form, or they move on, is not as important to us as it is to you."

"Oh, so you're changing the game. One of the goals in life on this planet, it seems to me, is about living as long as you can, avoiding illness, wars, violence and even accidents. That's why my parents' premature deaths were so hard to accept. Everything in the newspaper seems to be about life and death, not about finding out *who* we are."

"That's right, Ali. And survival is necessary for us to stay here on this planet—and our bodies are programmed for that. But imagine, Ali, what life would be like if survival was not our primary occupation."

"There wouldn't be fear, would there?" Ali responded. "So getting free from fear, I'm now beginning to see, isn't something we can practice; it's just a change of perspective. It's sort of like changing from looking through our eyes to looking through God's eyes or the eyes of the witness."

"Yes, Ali. And when you look through God's eyes, you won't feel like you're wearing tight shoes anymore."

"Okay. I think I understand. Thank you. Now, Vio, where do we go from here?"

"So far we've been to Haiti, Switzerland, Arizona and New York. The trip to Haiti was an extension of an old memory and the most recent three were in the present. Would you like another kind of destination for a change? Let's see if you're ready for this."

"Okay, but where will we be going?"

"Take my hand, I'll hold Layla, and we'll see."

Ali found herself standing in the clearing of a lush green forest, and a few feet away was Violetta, sitting by a tree. "Hi Vio. Everything seems different here. You seem to be as solid as I am. Are we in your dimension now? Are you solid in your dimension?"

"You could say that." And as soon as that was said, Vio appeared as a young woman with flowing red hair and a long flowered chiffon dress. Is this solid form to you?"

"What do you really look like? Are you just dressing as Vio for me?"

"Everything you have experienced in the material plane has been designed just for you by you. Don't try to figure it out; it will become clear later on.

"Maybe you will understand it better after I remind you of an experience you had at the dentist's office. Do you remember what happened when you were having your wisdom tooth pulled in 1973?"

"Yes Vio. I remember it very vividly. After they gave me nitrous oxide, I found myself on the ceiling, looking down at myself in the chair."

"What were you wearing on the ceiling?"

"A white blouse and dark slacks."

"Why weren't you naked? Why weren't you thinner, or why didn't you correct the nose that you felt was too big when you saw it from the ceiling?"

"How did you know that?" Ali asked in amazement.

Vio smiled at her question. "Don't be frightened. I know what I need to know. Just answer the question. Who decided how you would appear?"

"I don't know who decided what I was wearing, I just was."

"And was it appropriate to the situation?"

"Of course, no question."

"Well then, how I appear to you is arranged by your needs. You want a wise old woman, you have her."

In the next moment, Vio returned to appearance that Ali had met at Rose Cottage.

"What about Layla?"

"She appears to you in the same way. She is part of your story, and so is everything else."

"I don't get it. Where are we? Are we in the future? Are we on another planet?" As she spoke, a chill went through her heart and shoulders. "I'm making this up myself. I'm making all of this up myself. Why am I doing this? What is the point?"

Suddenly the forest disappeared, replaced by a dark screen like a starless night sky.

"Vio! Where are you, Vio?"

"Do you want me to return? Do you want to re-create me?"

"Oh yes, please."

"Maybe this trip was a bit premature for you."

"What do you mean by that?"

"You didn't stay with the blank screen for very long—only about three seconds by my timing."

"What would happen if I had stayed there longer?"

"All I know is what happened. You stayed three seconds and called me (and yourself) back into existence. That's okay; that's like the rubber band being pulled out and then springing back to its original form. It will be that way for a while."

"And what will happen when it isn't? Will there be nothing forever?"

"That is the fear of your ego, the one who wants the show to go on indefinitely. Do you ever wonder how the show would look from the point of view of the one who watches?"

"I can't even imagine. Would I see buildings of crystal like Superman's Fortress of Solitude? Could you please show me?"

"I don't know if you're ready for this. Are you sure? It may blow your mind."

"I'm sure. Blow my mind!"

"All right, hold my hand and you will view, as the observer, the world of creation, of your creation."

Ali grasped the formless form of Vio's hand and immediately saw a beautiful, radiant planet turning in a vast field of indigo, sprinkled with luminous stars. She and Vio were moving in slowly. As they came further in, Ali could see white, frothy material obscuring some portions of what looked like land masses and other parts that looked like seas. As they came closer still, she began to see some lights sparkling on the green areas. "Oh, this looks like a beautiful planet. Let's go there!" Ali began to discern more details, and it wasn't long before she recognized the outline of continents.

"Vio, I'm looking at the United States, and here's the East Coast, New York, and Manhattan Island. What is this? Is this a joke?"

"What do you mean? It isn't a joke. This is your beautiful creation. It's incredible in its diversity, don't you see?"

Ali snapped back into the view behind her eyes. She felt the pride of creation that was described in Genesis: ". . . and God saw that it was good." Yes, it was good, it was beautiful, all of it, every detail. Then they flew through the clouds, and the land looked like a design painted on silk, the light playing on the bends and folds. And there was rain, and the water bounced on the surfaces, on the ground, in the trees, on the umbrellas, on the shielded heads of people running for shelter. And then there was the rainbow, and then the night. It was all amazingly beautiful.

Still looking through God's eyes, as they came closer and closer in, Ali found herself, along with Vio and Layla, back in her loft in Chelsea. She noticed her favorite plate with a crack in it that she just couldn't throw away, the stuffed animal on her chair whose eye was hanging by a string, and she saw the beauty in their imperfection. She saw all of human life and the mark it made on the planet. She looked out her window and saw the people on the street, and marveled at how amazing they all were, all unique and all perfect. And when she adjusted her vision just slightly up a level, angels were flying everywhere, and there was light, even in the darkness. Light was emanating from everything.

"Whose creation is this?" Ali asked.

"It is yours when you are looking through the eyes of God. It is also yours when looking through your human eyes. The only difference is that when looking with your human eyes, what you see is altered by your personal interpretation. Which do you prefer?"

"Well, sometimes I like my personal interpretation, like when buy something new, or when I'm in love, or when I win a prize, or someone praises me, or when a baby is born. But I hate wars, poverty, rejection, failure, illness and death."

"Yes. So, Ali, through your human eyes there are lots of wonderful moments and beautiful things to see, and also lots of sad moments and ugly things to see. How do you feel about life on Earth when you are able to switch back to seeing through God's eyes?"

"Through God's eyes, I can see that nothing is always good or always bad, and that the dance between the two creates the beautiful patterns that give life its unique tastes and textures."

"So now, do you remember when you asked Ethan why he would choose to live sometimes in the manifest world? And what was his response?"

"Something about hot fudge sundaes for breakfast. I can see how the personal view shows the potential for amazing things to happen here on Earth. But in the view from God's eyes, everything is bathed in golden light and is already perfect, and there is nothing to do. But it's all God's view, Vio, the unity and the diversity. So, as Ethan said, it's all the same to him, and I can see now what he meant."

Ali collapsed into her comfy chair in a state of bliss. "It's all God . . . it's all God." She soon fell into a deep sleep.

When Ali awoke from her nap, the questions she hadn't been able to verbalize when she was with Vio came flying back. Although she was hesitant to ask because she feared Vio's disapproval, she felt it was important to understand what had been happening to her. Her desire to see Vio was so strong, in fact, that even though it was already late in the evening, Ali decided to show her strength of intention by driving to the lake. She even packed a nightgown and some toiletries, in case it seemed necessary to stay the night.

She left the condo at around seven o'clock. and arrived at Blue Swan Lake at nine (by her watch). She was no longer surprised that she had no recollection of the drive after entering the tunnel. She parked her car in the driveway, and since there was no moon in sight, she pulled out her flashlight and surveyed the area. Finding the coast clear, she opened the door with her key, walked into the parlor, sat down on an overstuffed chair, and let out an audible sigh. The house seemed empty, and she wondered if she'd done the right thing by driving out so late at night. She wondered if Vio was sleeping, or if she even needed sleep. It wasn't long before Vio came down the stairs—dressed appropriately in a nightgown and robe.

"My dear, what has brought you here, and at this late hour?"

"Vio, I've got lots of questions for you, and they just couldn't wait until morning."

Vio took a seat on the couch and offered Ali some tea and cookies.

"No thanks, Vio, not right now. I couldn't sleep, and I needed to talk about some of my experiences with you."

"What's on your mind, dear?"

"Well, Vio, since I've met you, I've had many visionary-type experiences; like the Kachina in Sedona, and the angels at the hospital. I have never read these descriptions in spiritual books, and I wonder if other people, in these same situations, would see the same things? You seemed very accepting when I described my visions, but I wonder if they were accurate?"

"Ah, a good point, and especially important if you ever teach or counsel people regarding their spiritual experiences. You see, my dear Ali, everything that you perceive—as Ali the personality—is absolutely subjective. Your mind, which must process all this information, is incapable of comprehending things beyond itself, and so it places energetic experiences in the contexts that it can understand.

"I'll offer you an example that might help to illustrate this point. Remember the night that you felt we were healing you? It happened on the second or third night we met."

"Yes. It looked like an MRI machine was going from my head to my toes, and then some kind of a machine was working on my neck area. I believe that was related to the disorientation that I've been experiencing since I started working with you."

"All right. Well, I must tell you that we don't have MRI machines here. And suppose we were working on people who didn't have that technology? Do you think their experience would match yours?"

"No, I guess that wouldn't be very likely," Ali answered.

"Ali, just know that while I am working with you in a human body, we must deal with your mind and your concepts. Now, I'm not saying you can't open your mind and accept new concepts, because you already have—but the mind will still have to make interpretations. It does that for your survival."

"So, does that mean that what I'm experiencing is not correct?"

"Yes and no. It is correct for you at this time, based on your beliefs. In another time in your development, you might experience the same things differently. What you saw was appropriate for the lesson being presented, but I will warn you now—and will continue to do so—that they are truly subjective. Please do not consider them the only *correct* experiences. Do not teach them to others, and do not judge or condemn others if their experiences look different from yours. It is all just a function of how the mind interprets things that it will never be able to comprehend."

"Well then, what does one teach?" Ali asked.

"There is only one thing to teach, you see. It is not to teach experiences; it is to teach that there is more to being than meets the eye. A teacher may gently nudge a student toward that understanding—or in the absence of a teacher, life will provide the impetus."

"So why are there so many teachings? I understand now why they're so different, but one could get really caught up trying to justify the differences, when, as you describe it, everything is subjective."

"Yes and even what I'm telling you now is subjective. I know, Ali, it has been a great joy for you in the past to study all the different expressions of God, and make comparisons of all the world's religions, but now you're in another phase of your learning. You know that everyone and everything is God, and that is the only teaching of any relevance for you now."

"But what about the others on the spiritual path? Is that the only teaching for everyone now?"

"As you know, there are many teachings on this earth plane, and many styles, many beliefs, and philosophies, and many forms of expression. And each and every expression is a piece of the Truth and is valid. People will be drawn to the teachings most appropriate to them in a particular moment in time, whether or not you agree with it.

"If you look back at your life, you know this is true. You see, Ali, until you can embody Truth, you will hear it through the mouths of many teachers; but there is really one teacher and one teaching in many forms. The Truth can come to you through a great sage, a false teacher, a loss, the transcendent beauty of nature, a line in a book, or even a song on the radio. We use whatever is available to us to bring you closer to your True Being. How does that feel, Ali?"

"It really does remove the need for judgment and comparison. So it's relaxing; but, in another way it's scary. I feel like there's no ground to stand on."

"Oh yes, an experience of Truth can also come from someone pulling the rug out from under you. So now that you have no ground to stand on, would you like to go to bed? I have the guest room ready for you."

Ali laughed in acknowledgment. "Yes, I think I have no other option. Thanks for being here for me this evening."

Ali walked over to the staircase, pulling herself up by the banister, and went directly to bed. She was so tired she forgot to ask Violetta whether or not spirit guides required sleep.

12

The Koan

Ali threw her legs over the edge of the bed and planted her feet on what she expected to be the hardwood floor of her loft bedroom. Instead, she felt a tickling sensation on the soles of her feet. She opened her eyes and looked around the strange room with its white shag carpet and four-poster bed. She remained disoriented until she recalled driving to the lake house with some burning question the previous night. Now the question—and its answer—had slipped her mind. She was amazed at how easily her mind could become disoriented. *How can I hope to comprehend ultimate reality when I can't even recognize a shag rug? And if I can't trust my mind, what can I trust?* That, she thought, would be a good question to pose to Violetta.

After washing and dressing, Ali was about to descend the staircase to the kitchen when she heard Violetta calling her from the open door of the turret room at the far end of the hallway.

"Good morning Ali. Let's have our coffee up here this morning."

Ali turned around and ran up the short stairway to the turret room, where she joined Violetta at the window overlooking the lake. The light sparkling on the surface of the water so delighted Ali that she was, for once, at a loss for words.

Violetta broke the silence. "If you can't trust your mind, what happens when you go beyond the mind? And can *you* go beyond your mind?"

Ali paused to think of an answer, but finally shrugged her shoulders and returned only a blank stare.

"It's a paradox, isn't it?" Vio turned and walked over to the desk, selected a book from the stack, and turned back toward Ali. "I do so love paradox. It is such an elegant teaching method, don't you know? So with your wide knowledge of comparative religions, what can you tell me about *koans*?"

"Well I know they're questions or teaching stories from, I think, the *Rinzai* School of Zen Buddhism in Japan, and they're teaching stories or riddles presented by the Master to the student. The student meditates on the koan and tries to come up with an answer. They say it usually takes years—maybe even ten years—before the student is able to resolve the paradox that the koan presents. That's about all I know. But I'll tell you right now, I don't want to take on a practice that takes ten years."

"Ten years or . . ." Vio snapped her fingers, "one moment." Vio flashed Ali a sly smile.

"Do you have a koan to read to me from the book in your hand?" Ali asked.

Vio turned the book over and showed Ali the cover, with the title *Zen Koans*, by Gyomay Kubose.

"Yes, that's exactly what I'd like to do. It's a teaching story that contains a number of questions for you."

Ali made herself comfortable on the couch as Vio read to her the following passage:

Bodhidharma and the Emperor Wu

Emperor Wu of China was a very benevolent Buddhist. He built many temples and monasteries, educated many monks, and performed countless philanthropic deeds in the name of Buddhism. He asked the great teacher Bodhidharma, "What merit is there in my good works?" Bodhidharma replied, "None whatsoever." The Emperor then asked, "What is the Primal meaning of Holy Reality?" Bodhidharma answered, "Emptiness, not holiness." The Emperor then queried, "Who, then, is this confronting me?" "I do not know," was Bodhidharma's reply. Since the Emperor did not understand, Bodhidharma left his kingdom.

Later, the Emperor related this conversation to an adviser, Prince Shiko. Shiko reprimanded him, saying that Bodhidharma was a great teacher possessed of the highest truth. The Emperor, filled with regret, dispatched a messenger to entreat Bodhidharma to return. But Shiko warned, "Even if all the people in the land went, that one will never return."

Vio flipped to the back of the book and remarked, "I see the answers to the koans are also included." She closed the book and held it in her hand. Ali rose from her seat, instinctively reaching for the book.

"You can grasp the book, but can you grasp the koan?" Vio remarked holding the book steadily.

Ali realized she had fallen into Vio's trap and tried to pull herself out. "Well, why would they include the answers then?"

"If one is not actively using the koan as a spiritual practice, it might be interesting to see the answers given by those who have achieved enlightenment through this practice. The mind, of course, will be tempted to memorize these answers—which is totally antithetical to the purpose of the koan. Do you understand what I am saying?"

Ali sheepishly dropped her extended hand and returned to her seat on the couch.

"Oh, Vio!" In an instant, Ali recognized the purpose of the lesson. "Each situation you have presented to me, so far, has been in response to a question—either spoken or unspoken. But, to be honest, I can't even remember any of the answers. But now I'm beginning to understand that it's the *process* of struggling with the question, not really the answer that holds the true value."

"Have you noticed yet that you will never find the answer within the belief system or concept that created the question? Just let that simmer—don't try to figure it out.

"Are you hungry, Ali? I think this would be a good time to break for lunch." Vio presented a simple meal, which they ate together silently. After lunch they returned to the turret room, at Ali's request.

"Okay Vio, so now I've had a lesson about koans, but I am still stumped by the question the Emperor asks of Bodhidharma, 'What merit is there in my good works?' and Bodhidharma answers, 'None whatsoever.' And then also, when the Emperor asks, 'What is the Primal meaning of Holy Reality?' and the answer is 'Emptiness, not holiness.' Assuming this koan represents some higher knowledge, these answers seem to be opposed to the teachings—in virtually all the religions—of doing good works and acting compassionately. So, based upon humanity's condition, is there anything we humans can do to better our condition? I suppose that is the real question."

"Indeed, it is an excellent question. Considering the answer of Bodhidharma to Emperor Wu, you have been taught in the opposite way, that you must work to purify your body, mind and spirit, that you must think positive thoughts, that you must fight evil. But the energy that you and others tend to access in order to do this work is the same energy you saw in the cancer group with your friend Janet, the Warrior. Remember how quickly she was burning out when she was trying to fix things with egoic energy?"

"Now I'm feeling even more frustrated. There are so many horrible things happening in the world now, with politics, starvation, natural disasters, AIDS, and people treating each other with such hatred and greed. I feel so guilty just being here enjoying life when these horrible things are happening. I think Bodhidharma's answer seems very selfish, or at best hopeless to me. How can you justify 'no merit' and 'no holiness'?"

"I know you're seeking an answer, but that, my dear, is not the issue. How can I possibly answer a question about these events? It is the quality of where you go for your answer that is most important. I would rather ask you about your feelings regarding this list you just told me . . . politics, starvation, disease, war. Tell me the feelings these subjects elicit in you."

"I think about all the pain that people perpetrate on each other, and how it's so difficult to make even a little difference, to bring even a little peace to the world. For every house Habitat for Humanity builds, how many remain homeless? I work hard to conserve water, and then I walk down the road and see a water main break with thousands of gallons of water pouring out into the street. I try to conserve energy by taking public transportation to save gas, and then there's a huge oil spill or an oilfield is bombed in Iraq. It seems so hopeless, Vio. How can I help?"

"Would you please tell me about the feelings that you've just described."

"Fear . . . pain . . . despair . . . hopelessness."

"And can a solution come from fear, pain, despair and hopelessness? If so, how?"

"The only thing I guess that comes from fear, pain, despair and hopelessness is more of the same."

"Yes, this is so. You've come upon a truth here. So can a person experiencing these emotions effect a change, a lasting change?"

"Maybe slightly, but the quality of the energy seems to go deeper and deeper, almost as if the attempts to make a change would dig a bigger hole. It's as if the energy needed to make a change is generated from the pain. But that's something, isn't it, Vio? Making something good from something bad?"

"Perhaps that has some limited beneficial effect, but I'm going to ask you later how you feel about this."

"Okay Vio, but before we go on our next journey, I have two more questions about the koan, okay?"

"Of course. What are they?"

"Well, if someone has the experience of knowing everything is emptiness, wouldn't they just sit on the couch and do nothing? I think I would. Maybe I'd watch some TV, but why bother with anything else. And the second one is that if there is no merit in good works, which is what it seems like from our discussion, it seems that you are teaching me something that is not about love at all. It seems pretty selfish and hopeless."

"I see how you might feel that way, but you won't understand the answer until you experience it yourself. I believe you've just created your own koan. I have something for you to do, and it's right outside in the back yard. I'd like you to mow the lawn."

"But it's winter! There's no lawn!" But as Ali was arguing her point, Vio walked her to the window facing the garden. Ali pulled back the drapes and saw that indeed there was a spring lawn, with trees and shrubs in bloom along the borders of the yard.

"Okay, why am I surprised? Of course it's spring in your garden. But I still don't understand why you want me to mow the lawn. Can't you do that with your thoughts, the way you planted the flowers along the front walkway, and cleaned away the cobwebs?"

"You'll see the answer to that as well."

Vio took Ali outside to the back of the house. It was a medium-sized yard, surrounded by trees and shrubs, bordered by a low stone wall. Ali noticed that there was a stone statue of the *Kamakura Buddha*, sitting at the foot of a beautiful oak tree that stood at the center point of the back wall. Vio showed her an old push lawn mower sitting just outside the back door, and disappeared into the house. Ali felt confused, but as she reluctantly began to push the rickety old machine back and forth across the grass, the koan came into her mind. *If everything is emptiness, why am I mowing the lawn?* By the time the lawn was finished, Ali had asked the question more than a hundred times. She was just about to return to the house when, to her surprise, the Buddha statue seemed to respond; and although the answer didn't come in words, the meaning was clear.

If everything is emptiness, why am I mowing the lawn? In that moment, Ali was again invited into the void. This time she allowed herself to fall deeper and deeper into the blackness, until she was completely dissolved. She had no idea how long she stayed in that space—although Vio later told her it was just about an hour. The state was indescribable. She could say only that at some point there was a shift, and all of a sudden, everything in creation came spilling forth from the void. She felt that she was experiencing the birth of the world. Her mind could not encompass the magnificence she was witnessing. And then she was born into the manifestation, loving and appreciating every detail, every ant, every leaf, dead or alive, the smell of the grass, the many shades of green, the petals of the roses, and the aphids chewing on the leaves.

As she came further into normal consciousness, Buddha explained to her that the teaching about the void was necessary so that she would empty out all her concepts and beliefs. Once she could truly experience the void, she would see that nothingness held the potential for everything, and only then could she fully experience creation. Ali gazed around the yard. The grass, the shrubs and the trees all were glowing. She then asked the Buddha aloud, in all earnestness, "Knowing all this, why am I mowing the lawn?" And the response came to her instantaneously, out of her own mouth: "Why not?"

When Vio wandered out to watch, Ali was radiant and joyful, absolutely delighting in her gardening task. "How is the mowing coming?"

"It is what it is, it's wonderful, it's perfect!"

Ali returned the mower to its place by the door, but when she turned to look back at the lawn she had just mowed, she was surprised to see the entire yard covered with snow. Her attention was drawn to the far end of the yard, where the stone Buddha sat in a position of total peace, cradling a dead oak leaf in his lap.

"How do you feel seeing your efforts of the last few hours covered with snow in one moment?" Vio asked.

"Surprised, but I have to admit I don't regret a moment of mowing the lawn. I don't even miss the flowers and the shrubs. And the dead leaf in Buddha's lap is as beautiful as an entire spring garden."

"Indeed." Vio smiled and patted Ali on the back. "Would you like to answer the questions you posed to me earlier?"

"Okay. Could you remind me of the question?"

"Certainly. I'll tell you exactly what you said. You asked, 'If someone has the experience of knowing everything is emptiness, wouldn't they just sit on the couch and do nothing?' That's the first one. What answer would you give now?"

"Now that I've had an experience of emptiness, I know, from deep inside, that emptiness is just the potential for everything. And when actions come from that place, they aren't from my ego, they're from the Creation itself. I can't imagine that would be a passive energy for very long."

"And your second question was, 'If there is no merit in good works, which is what it seems like from our discussion, it seems that you are teaching me something that is not about love at all. It seems pretty selfish and hopeless.' I believe that's exactly what you said."

"Well, Vio, I see that there was a misunderstanding of the word 'merit' on my part, because if you were to ask me 'Who deserves the merit for mowing the lawn?' I would have to say 'No one,' because *I* didn't mow the lawn. So the koan wasn't about merit at all; the koan was about *who* does the action."

"And how would that apply to your question about social action?" Vio asked.

"When I started to mow the lawn, I was in a place of reaction and resistance. That was an egoic attitude. I surely could have mowed the lawn in that mood, but I would not have enjoyed myself. I probably would have done a poor job of it and been tired at the end. But after the experience of the void, the lawn just *got mowed.* Any social action done from that place would have to be more effective, and there would be energy and enthusiasm because the action would be originating from the source. And there wouldn't be attachment to the results, as I noticed when I saw my work covered with snow in the next moment. It really didn't matter. The joy was just in moving in harmony with the Universe, according to its plan. And I expect social action can be done very elegantly from that place—and I'm certain there are people in the world doing just that, and in a very quiet but effective way. Didn't Jesus say something about not letting the left hand know what the right hand is doing? That's how it would feel—to not even know you're doing good works, because you're just moving with the flow."

Violetta nodded her head in approval, and continued. "And finally you said 'It seems that you are teaching me something that is not about love at all. It seems pretty selfish and hopeless.' What have you to say about that after your experience in the garden?"

"I found that it's the opposite. It is totally about Love, everything comes from Love, everything *is* Love. There is nothing more to say."

"Well, Ali, since there is nothing more to say, let's go back inside where it's warm."

13

More Questions

Ali woke up in the bedroom of the lake house to the sensation of Layla licking her ear. What a lovely way to awaken, she thought. And there was something very comforting about this old house, with its embroidered bedspread, flowered wallpaper and shaggy rug. For a moment she saw the entire setting as an elaborate construction created just for her; or perhaps it was her own mind creating a container for otherwise incomprehensible happenings.

She was enjoying the morning light streaming through the sheer curtains, and had started to fall back to sleep when she heard Violetta calling for Layla from the hallway. The dog turned her attention to the source of the sound and wagged her tail.

"She's in here with me. Come on in," Ali answered.

Violetta entered the room by way of the door. Ali appreciated the normality of that simple act, knowing that Vio and Layla could have just as easily made their entrance *through* the door. She also assumed that inter-dimensional beings didn't need to eat, although there was always a dog food bowl and water by the back door—at least whenever she was around.

"Good morning, Vio. Thanks for all this, by the way."

"For what?"

"For manifestation, I guess."

"That is *your* doing as well as mine." Changing the subject, Vio asked, "Did you have a good sleep last night?"

Back to normality, Ali thought. She responded that she could not recall a more satisfying sleep or a sweeter way to awaken. But there was still that nagging question that always came to mind whenever Violetta appeared.

"Every day I ask you a question, and through the experiences of the day, I come to some understanding. But then when I try to reconstruct later what happened, I can never remember the answer."

"I will be happy to shed some light on your question." Vio replied. "The reason you remember only your questions but not the answers is very simple. The part of you that remembers and tries to codify what you've learned is a part of the mind that has not *experienced* the answers. Do you understand what I'm saying?"

"Could you say more about the mind? It's still not entirely clear."

"Surely. Each day you have received the answer, but it is experienced on another dimension, with another part of your being. The logical part of the brain—the one that still exists in the world of opposites, believes it's vulnerable and that it can die, and it interprets reality from that standpoint. When you have experiences that transcend the mind and body, they are incomprehensible to that part of the brain. That's why it keeps asking the same questions again and again."

"Will it ever change? Is there any hope for me?" Ali wondered aloud.

"I believe there is. Some day the mind will just give up. It will finally recognize that it is only a small part of something immense, immortal, and beautiful beyond comprehension. But know also, Ali, that the mind is not to be discounted—it's to be valued and experienced."

"But isn't it the mind that holds the ego in place? I want to get rid of all those negative messages that keep running through my head. Isn't that the goal?"

Vio walked over to the door. "Follow me now. I have something to show you in the turret room."

Still in their bathrobes, they walked toward the narrow staircase to the upstairs tower. Once inside, the door closed gently behind them, and Vio turned toward the bookshelf to pick out a well read book with a ragged cover. Ali could just make out the title, *A Year with Rumi; Daily Readings*, translated by Coleman Barks.

Vio began turning the pages and stopped when she found the poem she was looking for. "Here it is. This poem on page 366 is the reading for November 22."

"That's the day I won the raffle—what a coincidence!"

Vio just smiled. "You haven't the slightest idea of the magnificence of this orchestration. When you notice a coincidence, or have a premonition or an experience of *déjà vu*, you're just getting a glimpse beyond the veil. It's all there, already complete, beyond time and space. You'll see."

"Okay. So what is the subject of this poem?"

"Oddly enough, Ali, it's called 'Guest House,' but it's not really about a house, it is about being human."

Ali took the book from Violetta's translucent hands and read aloud.

The Guest House

This being human is a guest house
every morning a new arrival.

A joy, a depression, a meanness,
some momentary awareness comes
as an unexpected visitor.

Welcome and entertain them all.
Even if they are a crowd of sorrows,
who violently sweep your house
empty of its furniture,
still, treat each guest honorably.

He may be clearing you out
for some new delight.

> The dark thought, the shame, the malice,
> meet them at the door laughing,
> And invite them in.
>
> Be grateful for whoever comes,
> because each has been sent
> as a guide from beyond.

"What do you make of this, Ali?"

"It reminds me of the feeling I had when I saw the Buddha holding the dead leaf, encompassing everything—positive and negative—or the tarot card of the High Priestess sitting between the two pillars of *Boaz* and *Jakin*."

"Excellent. It also offers insight, Ali, about how to recognize when the ego is in control of your consciousness. If you're experiencing resistance or judgment, the ego is active—even if it tells you it is resisting ego."

"So are you saying that the part of me that's *trying* to be spiritual is really the ego in disguise?"

"You might call it that. That's a very valid description."

"So then the only solution is to embrace everything—which is automatic when I'm looking from the higher perspective."

"Yes, that's the idea—"

"But why doesn't it stay with me? Each new day there is another fear and another falling into the belief that there will never be another experience of Truth available to me."

"Don't be hard on yourself. This is the human condition that Rumi addresses so beautifully. It's time for you to embrace your 'white cow.'"

"Embrace my white cow? What's a white cow?"

Violetta took *A Year With Rumi* from Ali's hands, turned to page 130 and handed the book back to her. "You can read this one silently, if you like."

A Small Green Island

There is a small green island
where one white cow lives alone, a meadow of an island.

The cow grazes 'till nightfull, full and fat,
But during the night, she panics
and grows thin as a single hair.
What shall I eat tomorrow? There is nothing left.
By dawn the grass has grown up again, waist-high.
The cow starts eating and by dark the meadow is clipped short.

She's full of strength and energy, but she panics
in the dark as before and grows abnormally thin overnight.
The cow does this over and over,
and this is all she does.

She never thinks, This meadow has never failed
to grow back. Why should I be afraid every night
that it won't. The cow is the bodily Soul,
The island field is this world where that grows
lean with fear and fat with blessing, lean and fat.

White cow, don't make yourself miserable
with what's to come or not to come.

Ali held the book to her heart for a moment and then placed it on the table beside her.

"I guess I'm not as unique as I thought. So this is the truth for everyone. We live in-between realities, going back and forth from one state to the other, never remembering the truths we have just experienced. Is that the best we can do while we have bodies? Is this a life sentence?"

Vio looked at Ali with such compassion it almost melted her. Ali felt, just from that glance, that she was being embraced by the most loving of all mothers.

Vio asked, "Who is this unwelcome visitor today? Show me who it is and what he's done to you."

"Sometimes I worry that our survival as a species is on the line. Crazy people have the bomb, and the people in power don't seem to care about the damage they are causing to the planet and the peril they're putting us all in. And I'm not talking about cleaning out the furniture—this is the whole, the whole thing, life itself. And what can I do about it? I remember how hopeful we were in the '70s, and now everything we worked for is being reversed—it's as if our generation didn't accomplish anything."

"Yes, we are aware of these happenings within your story." Vio responded, in a detached manner.

"And what are you doing about it?" Ali fired back.

"What do you think we're doing about it? Do you have any ideas?"

"Well you're helping us by teaching us about the different dimensions. But if all of it doesn't matter, why are you even bothering to help?"

"Aha!" Vio answered. "For the same reason I am wearing a bathrobe and opening and closing the doors. Within your reality you asked for help, so within your reality we respond in kind."

"You mean you're helping me in the way I imagine you can help me?"

"In some ways you are correct. We've spoken about this concept before. Do you remember what happened in your martial arts class when you were doing a very difficult bowing practice, and your nose started bleeding?"

"Yes, but how do you know about that?" Ali asked.

"We know all about your dream, dear. Do you remember the incident?"

"Yes, of course. My nose was bleeding, and I didn't want to discontinue the practice because the whole purpose was to persevere under any circumstances, to suppress my body's desire to stop. So I made a plea to the universe to stop my nose from bleeding, and I said that I would continue the bowing practice even if I bled all over the floor."

"Yes, and then what happened?"

Although Violetta obviously knew the end of the story, Ali continued. "After already discarding two tissues completely soaked with blood, I blew my nose with a third tissue, and when I looked at it, it was as white as snow, no blood whatsoever, and I was able to complete the practice. So I asked and received help from the universe. How does that relate to what you are telling me?"

"In the large scale of things, did your nosebleed really matter?" Vio asked.

"I can see today that it doesn't really matter whether or not I can control a nosebleed—but then why did you assist me?" Ali asked, shaking her head in confusion.

"Within your dream that is what was very important to you. Why did we do that? Because you asked. It's as simple as that."

"You mean it didn't mean I persevered over my body?"

"If you think so, you did."

"I received praise for it from my martial arts teacher."

"Isn't it all just so delightful? You set up tasks, spiritual tasks, and then you achieve them, and then you move on to the next ones."

"You're sounding very cynical, Vio."

"I'm sorry if it sounds cynical from where you sit, but it's very delightful for us. Remember the play of life is just God experiencing God through different bodies, and in different circumstances."

"I feel like I'm putting you on the defensive. I don't want to do that, Vio. I just want to know what this is all about. And if it's about nothing, why are we doing it? I don't feel like I'm doing this willingly, but I must be. I just don't feel capable of making all this up, with all this detail. I'm just not that imaginative."

"Have you ever had a dream that was very detailed? Did it have backgrounds and characters and actions and tension and thinking and speaking?"

"Yes, of course." Ali answered.

"And who do you think made that up?"

"Now I'm even questioning that. Maybe I don't even make up my dreams? Everything suddenly seems to be unraveling."

"Get up out of that chair. I'm taking you to a Broadway show. I feel there's something you need to see. It will provide a glimpse, a preview of the end of the story."

"A preview of the end of the story? What story? What are you talking about?"

"I'll show you—although you probably won't understand what you're seeing. I'm going to show you the end of the play before you live the second act. I feel, somehow, that it will help you to continue on."

"Okay, I trust you. Let's go see the end of the story."

In the next moment, they were standing in the lobby of a beautiful old Broadway theater. Ali was wearing an elegant floor-length black dress with a white satin stole, rhinestone-studded shoes and carrying a silver purse. Vio looked equally glamorous, and, Ali noticed, a bit younger than she usually appeared. She also wore a long gown, but with a velvet stole. As they walked by a dark glass door, Ali took a quick glance—as people often do when not wanting to appear vain. When she saw no reflection, she laughed at herself for expecting that they were visible. She thought it was a shame that she looked so sophisticated; and yet no one could see her but Vio. Well, at least she could enjoy her invisibility. But when she tried to walk through the door to the theater, she was stopped by both the door and Violetta.

"Not just yet, Ali. Not even while you're invisible."

"Oh please, could I just take a peek?" Ali assumed they were waiting for the scene to end, before entering the theater.

"Oh, all right, but just for a moment."

Ali opened the door a crack and looked inside. "The theater is almost full. This must be a popular play."

"Close the door now, Ali. We'll have to wait just a little bit longer."

Ali took one more look at the stage, and then stepped back and let the door close behind her.

After what seemed like an eternity, Vio motioned to Ali that now was the time to enter. She pushed open the door for Ali and directed her to two empty seats at the end of row Q—which appeared empty, even after they were seated. She asked Violetta what would happen if someone tried to sit in their laps. Vio put her finger to her lips and pointed to the stage.

Ali looked up at the stage, but was disappointed to see that the play was over. "Vio, these are the curtain calls. We've missed the entire play!"

"I can see how you might think so, but trust me, you haven't missed a thing."

"But they're taking their bows."

"Yes, I told you I would be showing you the end of the play. Enjoy it now, and we'll talk about it later."

Ali returned her attention to the stage, and whispered to Violetta, "Some of these actors look very familiar. Look, there's Ethan, the Sedona guide. I didn't know he was an actor. Oh, and there are ten women walking forward from the back of the stage and taking their bows. Aren't those the women from the breast cancer group? And there's the mother, daughter and guide from Switzerland, and they're all holding hands. This is pretty strange."

But it was about to get a lot stranger. Next onto the stage, to a huge round of applause, walked Violetta and Layla, visible to everyone, and behind them came a woman with long silver hair who looked a lot like Ali, only quite a bit older, exuding a kind of radiance that Ali intuitively knew didn't come from the spotlight. She received lots of applause.

The next person to come out on the stage was an older man in a tuxedo. He was very tall and distinguished, with a full head of wild white hair. He had a presence about him that led her to believe he might be the conductor or maybe the producer. She knew she'd never seen him before.

Ali looked down for a moment while she opened her purse to find a tissue, and when she looked up again at Vio, she realized she was no longer in the theater, but was seated beside Vio on the cozy overstuffed couch in the living room of the lake house.

"What just happened? What did I just see?"

"You saw the very end of the show, my dear, but you saw actors you have yet to meet and scenes you have yet to play."

"I wonder what I missed."

"Have faith that it will be good. The audience left quite satisfied, uplifted even, and the actress who played you carried a light within her that I have never seen on a Broadway stage before."

"Has it been reviewed?"

"Oh, yes. Here's the review." Vio picked up a newspaper from the coffee table and read a part of the review for Ali. "It says here, and I quote: 'This play is a story about life on Earth.

Alicia Morgenstern, the main character, asks the questions we are afraid to ask, and the answers will astound you. It has drama, humor, tragedy, and lots of heart, with an uplifting spiritual message. It is an evening on Broadway that I guarantee will change the way you see the world.'"

"But, Vio, why couldn't I see the play now? I don't understand."

"Ali, you couldn't see the play yet because in your world it hasn't yet been written. But I can assure you that it will be wonderful. This you know from the reception and the reviews. I can tell you that it is worth your while to stay and complete it.

"Now you'll need a good night's sleep after the events of today. As you have just seen, you have a full life ahead of you. Good night, Ali."

Ali began wondering what Vio meant by that, as she put her head on the soft down pillow. She was asleep before she could finish the thought.

ACT II

14

On Her Own

Ali opened her eyes and reached over the side of bed to feel if Layla was there. *Ah, they're still here . . . good,* she thought. She threw on her robe and went downstairs to the kitchen, with Layla following closely at her heels. The coffee cup she expected to find on the table was missing, but in its place was an espresso machine. Ali didn't want to accept the truth of what she was seeing, and ran through the house calling out to Vio, looking in all the rooms. *How could this be? Layla is here, so where is Vio? She must be here somewhere.* It was only when she threw open the door to the turret room that she realized her premonition was correct. On the desk sat a small pink note written in flowery script. She picked it up. It smelled like roses, and on it were the words, "Enjoy your new home. Remember me. Remember who you are. I am you. Violetta."

Ali wondered if the old woman had really meant to say, "I am yours." Then she read the postscript on the bottom of the page. It said: "P.S. Layla wants to stay with you. She will be your companion on Earth for as long as you live. Directions for the new coffeemaker are on the counter."

After her breakfast, Ali packed up her few items, put Layla in the car, and began the drive to the city. As she backed out of the driveway, she realized that she was not the same person who drove to the lake in the middle of the night with the burning questions that had disturbed her sleep. She felt exuberant now, as if limitless possibilities were open to her—and there was nothing she *needed* to do, and nothing more she *needed* to know.

As the car emerged from the Lincoln Tunnel into the light of day, New York City never looked so vibrant and new as it did on this brisk December morning.

Since Vio had exited her life, Ali assumed things would get back to *normal,* but as she turned the key in the lock of her loft, the next act of the play was about to commence without so much as an intermission.

Ali was turning the handle on her apartment door when the neighbor across the hall poked her head out of her door and whispered to Ali in a soft but harsh voice, "You know dogs aren't allowed in this building, don't you?"

Thinking fast, Ali responded without much hesitation, "Oh no, this dog belongs to an old lady I visit almost daily. She had to leave town unexpectedly for a few days, so I'm just dog-sitting. The puppy isn't used to being alone."

"Oh, thank goodness. We did allow small dogs when we first went condo, but with the barking at all hours of the night, and the messes in the hallway, the condo association ended up passing a no dogs rule. As you know, this is an exclusive building, and we can't have it smelling or looking as if no one cares."

"Oh, I certainly know what you mean." As the woman pulled her head back into her apartment, Ali noticed that Layla was no longer on the end of the leash. *Ah, still moving between dimensions*, Ali thought. Well, that's useful, for sure. And with a sigh of relief, Ali guided invisible Layla through the open door. As soon as they heard the door across the hall slam shut, Layla reappeared.

As she put down her suitcase on the table and took in the view of Fifth Avenue, Ali wondered about the role the lake house would have in her life, now that Vio was gone. It was winter, and Blue Swan Lake was a summer and weekend community, so she decided that she would keep her center of activity in New York for now. She regretted that she hadn't remembered to take some books from Violetta's wonderful library—especially the translations of Rumi and Kabir.

She walked over to her desk to check her mail, and it was then she noticed that one of her bookcases—which had been empty the previous day—was full to overflowing with books from Violetta's turret room, including volumes by Ramana Maharshi, Rumi, Kabir, Hafiz, Meister Eckhart, Bankei and others. As she read over the titles, however, she sensed a subtle change in her relationship with the books.

For the past thirty years, Ali had called herself—with pride—a "spiritual seeker," and had always believed that the end of her search would come when all her questions were finally answered. Every new book she bought held the promise that this one would have the answer, that this one would end her quest. And although she had read many inspiring books, none ever fulfilled that promise. But today, sitting alone in front of some of the greatest writings of the world, she realized that the impulse to seek was oddly missing. She was surprised to find that the seeking hadn't ended in the way she'd expected—when the questions were answered. Instead, the seeking ended when the questions *dissolved*. And it hadn't happened with a burst of energy, or even a moment she could put her finger on. She just didn't see the point of looking anymore. She couldn't even remember what she had been looking for.

The only question she could come up with was about what to do next, and the answer came easily. She would take Layla for a walk. Not knowing whether inter-dimensional dogs pooped, she decided to take a few plastic bags along, just in case. She put on her coat and was about to attach the leash when she realized that walking a leash without a dog might look strange, even in New York City. So, foregoing the collar, Ali pulled the door closed behind her, and she and Layla headed for the park. They had a nice walk for about twenty minutes, and then, since the weather was quite chilly, Ali decided it was time to go home and have a nice hot cup of coffee.

As they approached the door to apartment 5B, Ali heard some unusual sounds coming from inside. Before she could decide her next move, Layla left her side, and Ali saw her jump right through the front door. The next thing she heard was a loud and violent barking sound, and in a split second, a man wearing a ski mask threw open the door and tore out of her apartment, dropping a bag of stolen goods as he ran down the hall. Chasing him was a huge Rottweiler, foaming at the mouth. The thief turned around to see if the dog was gaining on him, pulled open the door to the stairway, and made his getaway. At that point, Layla returned to her Terrier form and sat obediently beside Ali, who was taking some deep breaths to get her heartbeat back to normal. "Thanks, Layla. I think I might have underestimated the abilities of an inter-dimensional dog."

Ali picked up the bag and re-entered the apartment to assess the damage. She was relieved to find that nothing was broken or seriously disturbed beyond open drawers and scattered clothing. In the bag was some gold jewelry taken from her dresser and some old prescription medications from her medicine cabinet.

She doubted he would return to her place again, thanks to Layla, so she decided against calling the police, since she couldn't imagine how she might explain the Rottweiler's part in the scenario. Inter-dimensional existence came with a set of unique challenges, she realized, that didn't always correspond with the rules and regulations of the earth plane. Ali recalled the theater review that Violetta had read to her the night before. *Didn't it say something about how the play would "change the way you see the world?"*

Ali's thoughts were interrupted by the vibration of her cell phone in her pocket. When she saw the name "Cathy" on the caller I.D., she realized that she had been out of communication with her friends—and the *real world*—for over two weeks. She remembered that Cathy's daughter Eve was due to have a baby and that she had offered to be present at the birth. She eagerly answered the phone and, as she suspected, Eve was at the hospital just around the corner, and her cervix was already five centimeters dilated. She was planning a natural birth and was in one of the family-oriented labor rooms in the labor and delivery wing. Ali was out the door while still speaking on her cell phone to Cathy and ran the two blocks to the hospital.

Ali had attended the births of many of her friends as a *dula,* or coach, and always considered childbirth a miraculous event, but she wondered how it would be today, now that she was able to see reality from different perspectives. She sensed that the best advice would be to stay open and flow with whatever was happening. She heard an inner voice saying, *Yes, go with your intuition. You're on your own now, and it's your best connection.*

She arrived at the hospital when Eve was fully dilated and was beginning to push. This was the most difficult part of the labor for the mother, but the most exciting for the family and the coach, because it was the time when the head would start to crown. Fortunately for Eve, the second stage was short. It took only three pushes for the baby to fully emerge. As the baby was placed on Eve's stomach, her husband and mother began the ooh's and aah's that always accompany the miracle of birth. Ali stood to the side and turned her attention inward to see if there was anything she was required to say or do. But before she could finish her thought, she found herself backing out of the room and standing by the open doorway of the adjacent labor room. She intuitively knew that, for some reason unknown to her, she was here to witness another—and very different—birth.

In this second room, there was a great commotion, as emergency procedures were in progress. This second baby was being born with the cord wound tightly around its neck. The baby was not receiving the oxygen it needed, and the doctor was unable to remove the cord quickly enough. The beautiful light experience had turned into a dark moment of intense grief, as the mother screamed, over and over again, "Is my baby okay? Is my baby okay?"

They were able to revive the tiny blue body, but rushed him off to the intensive care nursery. The mother, with arms reaching toward the empty doorway, was still screaming for her baby. The father crawled into the bed and held her tightly. "We'll make it though this. If our baby lives, we'll do everything in our power to show him how much we love him, no matter what. And you will always know how much I love you now, in this moment, and always."

Ali moved away from the doorway and found herself at the entrance to a third labor room—again as a witness. In this room there was a young teenaged girl, her parents and a boyfriend, equally young. Standing to the side was a couple in their early thirties, holding hands and watching the monitor by the mother's head, as it registered the vital signs of the unborn child with each contraction. Ali soon deduced that this baby was being put up for adoption, and the couple—while trying to remain unobtrusive—was watching the heartbeat of the baby that would soon become *their* child. The girl giving birth was screaming, "Get this thing out of me! Cut me open! Get it out!" But in the final moments of pushing, she was as single-minded as any mother of any species on the planet. And when the baby was born, her first instinct—as with all mothers—was to hold it, count its fingers and toes, stroke it and nurse it. Knowing this, the nurse quickly showed the baby to her from afar and took it out of the room to clean it. The new adoptive parents followed the nurse into the other room where the baby was washed, assessed, and placed into the waiting arms of her new mother. If Ali ever needed a definition for "ambivalence," this was it.

Although Ali had been the witness of three very different births, she hadn't experienced any change in her perception until she found herself being moved again. But this time she was hovering above the Labor and Delivery Wing, looking down into the three rooms, simultaneously, as if looking into a doll house.

In the first room, she saw her friend Cathy's daughter Eve, rejoicing in a normal birth of a healthy little girl. she would name *Shanti*—the Hindu word for peace. And although the birth was perfect, Ali was shown a brief flash into the near future which indicated that this beautiful birth experience was not enough to keep an unstable relationship together. Indeed the stress of the additional being, which the now-elated parents hoped would bring them closer together, would cause them much pain in the future, as they would be fighting for custody within the next two years.

In the second room, the little boy would survive but would have the difficult life of a child soon to be diagnosed with cerebral palsy. The promises the father made on that seemingly disastrous day would be kept all their lives. The family was full of love and faith, and the child, although handicapped, was free to express his beautiful soul from the moment of his birth until his early death at age forty. In those short years, he became a man of great sensitivity, a musician and a scholar, and inspired many students to overcome their disabilities and fulfill their destinies rather than fall into despair. His parents never considered themselves victims, and therefore he learned by example to see his life, and every life, as valuable and beautiful. In the end, the family and the world benefited from the experience that had seemed so tragic to Ali just moments earlier.

And in the third room, a little girl was adopted, and the teen mother, unknowingly, gave up the only child she would ever have. As a result of this decision, in her future life there would always be a tinge of sadness and regret that would never completely leave her. It would, however, fuel a life of service to pregnant teenagers. She went into social work and wrote a book about her experiences from the depth of her heart. This ability to express herself and feel compassion for others in this same situation made her more accessible to the young adults she worked with. They believed her, and they trusted her because they felt the truth in her words. In her wisdom, she never pushed the teenagers toward any particular solution, but taught them, instead, to learn to live with their decisions and openly express their feelings, as she had.

Ali sighed as she took a last glance at the three rooms at once. She was awed and overwhelmed by the blinding light in all three rooms and the intense emotions experienced during each of the births. She saw that, regardless of what was to come, birth was an amazing miracle—it was another part of God coming into form. It was magnificent, and that was all she could see, and all she could feel.

During the walk home in the light snow, Ali began to feel the chill. She'd rushed out quite suddenly and hadn't dressed accordingly. The bodily discomfort was instrumental in bringing her attention back to the physical plane.

When she arrived home, Ali couldn't help but feel that there was something familiar about the events of this morning, like *déjà vu*. A memory of the trip to the theater with Violetta came into focus, and in her mind's eye she re-lived the moment when she took a quick peek into the theater—just before she was pulled away from the door. She remembered first having the impression that the theater was filled to capacity, but she also had a quick glimpse of the stage. She couldn't make sense of what she was seeing at the time, but now she recognized the set as being the three labor rooms, side by side. She wasn't sure if her mind was playing tricks on her, but this remembrance prompted her to turn on her laptop computer and do some research.

Now, what was the name of the play we went to see? And what was the name of the theater? She asked herself. As if the question was heard, she was directed to look, in her imagination, at the marquee as she and Vio had approached the theater. *"Yes, that was it! The play was called The Legacy of Violetta Rose."* She placed her fingers eagerly on the keyboard and started a search of the title, *The Legacy of Violetta Rose*, hopefully to find the review Vio had shown her. She found an English company that sold products called "Violetta Rose Water," and a young girl had a personal webpage with the name "Violetta Rose"—but no listing about the play, no indication that it ever existed. Perhaps it was a book first, she thought. She punched up a bookstore website and searched for a book called *The Legacy of Violetta Rose*, and again came up empty. How about *her* name? Maybe there was a reference to it that she might find if she searched for her own name. She did come up with a reference to a donation she had made, in the name of her parents upon their deaths. And there was a link to the Alzheimer's & Dementia Foundation website that listed her as the winner of a raffle held on November 22 for a summer home on Blue Swan Lake. Well, that was something she would certainly never forget. *But what about the play?* She wondered. *Was it my imagination, or was it a dream?*

It was time for what she called a "reality check." She looked around and saw she was sitting in a loft on Fifth Avenue, and that was no dream. But how did she get here? Did she perhaps buy it herself and by some trick of her imagination, or even insanity, conjure up the existence of a ghost named Violetta? Maybe this wasn't even her apartment. Well, if that was true, what was this dog doing here, sitting in her lap and nipping at her earlobe? Again she was experiencing a loosening of the comforting boundaries of reality she had been forced to release just over two weeks ago.

Okay, only one thing left to do, she thought. *First thing in the morning I will have to drive back out to the house and take another look.*

15

Return to the Lake

Layla, although reticent to use the elevator, responded with enthusiasm when Ali said, "Layla, let's go for a ride." She reluctantly followed Ali into the moving box down to the lobby; and together they rode back through the Lincoln Tunnel and out to Blue Swan Lake.

It was about eleven o'clock when they arrived. The house was still in pretty good shape, although there was some dusting to do to bring it up to the condition it was when Violetta was living there. Ali stopped off in the kitchen and made herself a cup of espresso with the machine that had been left for her. Cup in hand, she walked up to the turret room, with Layla playfully jumping at her feet. As she opened the door, the panoramic view of the lake caught her eye. Directly below the window sill, on the desk, she saw a stack of poetry books. Looking looked through the titles she found the volume she was looking for. She picked it up to have a better look. It was a beautifully bound volume with gilded pages and a swirling design of blues and purples on the cover that seemed hypnotic and somehow familiar. Above the design was the title *The Legacy of Violetta Rose*, and below it was her name, "Alicia Morgenstern." She cautiously opened the book to the title page and then turned the pages, finding chapters entitled "Florida," "Switzerland" and "Cancer Group." There was even one chapter called "More Questions." Then she saw a new title page with only the words "ACT II", and the chapters after that said "On Her Own" and then "Return to the Lake."

Before Ali looked further, she took a deep breath. This could be amazing, and she wanted to be centered as she read on. She had a habit of turning to the end of a novel to get a glimpse of how it would end—but when she turned to the back of this book, she found only empty pages. She flipped back through the book quite far until she found the last page that had printing on it. Tucked between the last printed page and the first blank one was a handwritten note on flowered notepaper that had the scent of roses. On it was written: "Ali, I am leaving this book for you. Consider it a journal of sorts. The rest of the story has yet to be written. This is your gift, and I encourage you to write, every day, your experiences of life on this planet, with all its joy and all its sadness. It is a journal, but will also serve as an instruction manual for people who, like you, are learning to live in two dimensions simultaneously; and it will help them to see the beauty and the Divine Purpose of this remarkable creation." It was signed in a very formal way, "Forever, Violetta Rose."

Ali put aside the note and looked at the last printed page. The words she saw written were as follows: "Ali put aside the note and looked at the last printed page. The words she saw written were as follows:"

She put the book in her purse to bring home to the loft. Her mind was filled with ideas, but she knew that this kind of book was not written by the mind. *Am I to be an author?* She mused. *No, not really, that doesn't seem right.* She determined she would just sit down at the end of each day and write what flowed from her pen. There was an odd mixture of anticipation, faith, and fear that no words would come; but she knew that nothing would dampen her determination to complete the assignment.

They arrived home after midnight, and Ali picked up the book to write. First she wrote the account of the finding of the incomplete journal. It was quite a revelation to realize that she would have to write the book before the play would ever be realized. *What did that really mean?* She thought. *Am I really going to write a play and have it performed on Broadway, or is my life the play?* And although this question was not answered, based upon her experiences of the previous two weeks, she had the patience to wait until the end. As she completed that thought, she realized, intuitively, that in the end, it wouldn't make a bit of difference.

16

The Police

Ali woke up and cautiously looked over at the bedside table to make sure the book was really there. It was. Paging through it, she noticed that the previous night's entry had been converted to the same print as the previous chapters. Her attention was drawn to the margin, where she noticed two small notes written in pencil. The first one said "Well done," and the other said "Pet Layla for me." This caused her heart to leap with pride and joy, knowing that Vio was still with her, monitoring her progress—although she felt awkward when she realized that everything she did, felt and thought would have to be included in the journal. She wondered if perhaps she could edit her writing to show herself in a better light; but an inner voice told her that would be impossible—and surprisingly that knowledge was reassuring.

Her thoughts were interrupted by a knock on the door. She looked through the peep hole and noticed two men looking back at her.

"This is the police. We're in the building investigating a rash of burglaries. I'm Detective Morrisey and this is Detective Minnelli."

"How do I know you're policemen? You're not in uniform."

"We're detectives, Ma'am . . . plainclothes detectives." The man who had identified himself as Detective Morrisey held up his ID card and badge to the peep hole in her door, where she could see them.

Ali opened the door and released the chain. "Would you like to come in?" she said. The two men filed into the apartment. Ali noticed that Detective Morrisey bore a slight resemblance to the man who had greeted her with the gun on that night she first visited Rose Cottage. She asked if he had any relatives at Blue Swan Lake, but he said he didn't. Detective Minnelli seemed to be checking something in the doorway, and she saw him pull a notepad from his pocket.

"I'm Alicia Morgenstern. I just moved in here two days ago, Saturday." She saw the second policeman taking down everything she was saying.

Detective Morrisey began the questioning. "We're investigating a rash of burglaries in the building. One of your neighbors indicated that you might have had a problem here." She wondered, for a split second, if it was the same neighbor who had complained about the dog, and wondered what else this neighbor might have seen—but brought her attention back to the question.

"Yes, Sir, I went out for a walk, and when I returned I think I caught him in the act. As soon as I opened the door, he ran out, dropped his bag, and ran down the stairs."

The second detective, with pad in hand asked Ali, "When did this event happen?"

"It was Saturday, the day I moved in."

"Why didn't you call us?" Morrisey asked. For a moment, Ali felt that he might have some suspicions about her.

"Well, to be honest, I didn't want to get involved. He dropped the bag as he ran away, and he didn't get anything, so I just figured I didn't need to bother you with filing a report."

"It is possible he did get away with something that you haven't noticed yet—maybe jewelry, drugs, money, or checkbooks. Also, there have been some other burglaries in the building, so we would like your help." Ali dropped her head in a kind of nod that indicated shame and willingness in the same gesture.

"Did you get a good look at him?"

"Well, officer, he was wearing a ski mask, but I could see his hair. It was kind of dirty blonde, stringy and pretty long. It was hanging out the back of his ski mask. He was about five-ten I'd guess, lanky body, probably a teenager."

"Do you remember what he was wearing?" Minnelli asked.

"I think jeans and a leather jacket and gloves, hiking boots, I think."

Detective Morrisey asked the next question. "Miss Morgenstern, did you notice how he entered the apartment?" As he was asking, Detective Minnelli spoke from where he was standing at Ali's door.

"Look here, the lock is tripped. Did you push the button in on the door?" he asked.

"Oh, I might have. I was only going out for a few minutes," Ali answered.

"You have a good lock here, Ma'am, but you need to use it whenever you go out."

Again Ali felt stupid, but she could sense the detectives were concerned about her safety.

They asked if she still had the bag and the items that were dropped, and she told them she had already laundered the pillow case which was the "bag" he used, and replaced the jewelry and medicines back where they belonged. And although she told them he was wearing gloves, Detective Minnelli asked her to retrieve some of the items for him to take prints, and he dusted the edges of the door and doorknobs as well. Satisfied that they had as much evidence as they could gather, they presented their cards, requesting that she call if she saw anything suspicious, or remembered anything else that might assist them in the case. They also reminded her to lock the door.

After the two policemen left the apartment, she took their cards and checked her desk for her checkbooks and extra checks, which were, thankfully, where she had left them.

Ali went into the kitchen and was about to put the kettle on the stove when the doorbell rang. At first she assumed it was the police with some more questions, so she opened the door leaving the chain engaged—to show them she was being more cautious. Instead, she was looking into the face of a boy who couldn't have been much older than sixteen. He had long blonde hair that probably hadn't been washed for quite some time. Her first thought was that he could have been her son. Her second thought was, thank God he wasn't, since he was obviously strung out on drugs.

"I'm sorry to bother you, Lady, but I was a witness to the robbery at your apartment . . ."

Ali knew she hadn't noticed anyone else in the hallway as the robber ran out, but allowed the boy to continue.

". . . and I saw this huge Rottweiler running down the hall, and then it disappeared into thin air. I'm beginning to think I'm crazy. I kinda wanted to ask you about it. I can't think of anyone else I can talk to."

"What's your name?"

"Jason."

Ali wasn't born yesterday, although she thought maybe part of her was. She knew that Jason—if that was his real name—

was the kid who robbed her, or who attempted to, and had been foiled by Layla's imaginative intervention. She didn't know why, but she felt it was safe to open the door and let him in. It reminded her of the feelings she had the first time she entered Vio's house. She knew it could be dangerous, with the gunman blocking her way, but beneath that feeling was a knowing that this was her destiny. She disengaged the chain lock and gestured for him to enter.

Jason seemed surprised at the invitation, but he shuffled in and looked around, trying to act as if this was the first time he'd seen her apartment. "Nice place you got here."

"Yes, thank you. Do you live in the building?" She thought better of that question as soon as it left her mouth.

"No, just visiting a friend here . . . you know, like I was the other day. But lady, I want to get right to the point. Am I crazy, or what?"

"Let me get you something to drink first, Jason . . . right? Coffee, tea, hot chocolate?"

"Hot chocolate's good." Ali went off to the kitchen area and continued talking as she heated the milk.

"I know times are really tough for kids your age. How old are you, about sixteen?"

"Yeah."

"The world's a lot more complicated now than it was when I was growing up. . . and that was tough enough."

"Yeah, it's really hard sometimes just to get up in the morning. I feel crazy. I hear people saying one thing and doing exactly the opposite. I used to think if I listened to people, parents, teachers, politicians, and did what they said, things would work out all right—but when I'm honest, I get beat up. When I tell the teachers in school some of my ideas, they tell me I'm crazy and send me to the school psychologist. Then, when I saw that dog yesterday, I thought maybe they're right. Maybe I *am* crazy."

"What kinds of things do you tell people that make them think you're crazy?" Her counselor persona couldn't resist that question.

"When I say what I'm *really* seeing, instead of what I'm supposed to be seeing."

"Oh, do you mean you have a different idea of what's true?"

"That too, but this is something else. Like sometimes when I'm upset about something, I can just sort of shut off my mind, and I rise up above the whole room and I see things in a really different way."

"Tell me more about that." She saw herself crossing her legs and resting her chin in her palm. *Old habits are hard to break*, she thought.

"Well, like maybe I'm having a fight with some guy about a really hot girl, and I'll be thinking I want to kill him to get him out of the way—but then when I go up on the ceiling, I see he's as scared as I am and he's just putting on an act for the girl, same as me. And then I kind of laugh at how we're all like stupid animals sometimes."

Ali nodded. "I think I have an idea about what you're getting at. And it's strange because often, even though you know all that is true, you still act like an animal. Like when you really want something really badly, like doing something really mean or dangerous, or even taking a drug that you know can addict you or even kill you—and you know absolutely you shouldn't do it, and yet you do. It's like we're living in two different dimensions at the same time."

"Wow, who are you?"

"Jason, I think there's a reason we've met. I want you to know you're not crazy. I'm not ready to talk about the dog yet, but I'd like you to come visit me tomorrow morning. Will you come back about ten?"

"Yeah . . . I'll be here."

"Just ring apartment 5B and I'll buzz you in, and I'll have some hot chocolate ready for you."

"Okay, see you tomorrow."

Ali showed him out the door and wondered what she could do or say that might help him get off drugs and recognize that he was special. She was eager to see what would happen tomorrow.

Ali spent the rest of the day organizing her new home, shopping to stock the refrigerator, especially with milk and chocolate syrup. As she finally sat down and began paging through some of the books Violetta had left her, Layla reappeared. It seemed that she had made herself scarce when Jason was around, just in case he recognized her.

Before bed, Ali took the journal into her lap and wrote her remembrances of the day, especially about Jason. She wrote her question down about whether she might play a part in his healing. Then she took a deep breath and reminded herself to trust, and fell asleep with the journal in her lap.

17

Jason Returns

Every morning since Violetta left, Ali woke up rehearsing what she would say when she saw her again. She would tell her how much she missed her, and how she almost believed she really wasn't going to return. But this morning, it was beginning to sink in that she really was on her own—with the exception of Layla, who was sleeping by the side of the bed. Ali took the journal from her bedside table to check if there were any additions. Her handwriting had again turned to print, and there was a question underlined with a star next to it. The question was: "I wonder what part I might play in Jason's healing?" She found another star in the right margin. Next to it, again in pencil, it said: "Who are *you*? That makes all the difference."

Ali had given Jason an open invitation, and so she wasn't surprised when at ten o'clock she heard a knock on her apartment door.

When she saw Jason through the peephole in the door, he didn't look well at all. As she ushered him in the door, she mentioned that he looked ill, but he just shrugged and changed the subject. "I'm really hurting a lot, and the only times I'm not hurting are when I'm on drugs or when I'm outside of my body. You talked yesterday about other dimensions. I want to know more about that. I want to go there with you."

"Jason, I have become aware, recently, that we are living on many levels simultaneously. From one level, everything that is happening here is taken very seriously. The body reacts from the place of survival—that's its job. But when the body recognizes something as potentially dangerous—whether it really is or not—it starts sending chemicals through the body that sometimes put it in an aggressive mood. 'Fight or flight' is what it's called. Do you follow what I just said?"

"Yeah. That's where I'm at *all* the time."

"I believe that's only partly true; because, you see, even when you're in that space, there's another part of you that isn't. You described that to me yesterday when you talked about being up on the ceiling, about being a witness."

"Yes, but what's the point? I'm still in pain most of the time. Can you teach me how to stay in that place you said is like a witness more?"

Ali decided to use another tactic. "Jason, do you know that on other planes there are beings who are caring about us and helping us?"

"That's what people say, but I don't feel very lucky."

Ali felt defensive with that remark—since she knew he was lucky to meet her and lucky that she didn't have him arrested—but she knew it wouldn't go down well if she challenged him yet. "Jason, I can tell you for sure that there are many people who have angels around them and don't see them."

"Can you see angels around me?"

"Well, honestly, I haven't looked." Ali tried to adjust her eyes, the way Vio had helped her before, but nothing changed. "Maybe we could do some kind of meditation together and then I'll be able to see more, and maybe you will also. Are you willing to try?"

"Sure. I don't have much to lose. How do you do it?"

Ali had led guided meditations when she taught childbirth preparation classes and in her Jungian therapy, but this time she decided to let the induction come *through* her so that it would be absolutely appropriate for Jason.

"Jason, I'd like you to lie down on the couch and relax, and as I speak you will begin to visualize your holy place. Your imagination will fill in the details. Is that okay with you?"

"Sure. But what is it supposed to look like?"

"It will look like however you see it. Whatever you see will be the perfect place."

"What if I can't see anything?"

"Can you dream?"

"Sure."

"Then you can see things with your mind's eye."

"My mind's eye, I like that. Okay, I'll try."

Once he was comfortable on her sofa, Ali began with a progressive relaxation exercise. When she felt that he was sufficiently relaxed, and his breath was slow and deep, she began to narrate a guided visual meditation. She started by having him imagine that he was in a field, engaging all his senses. He was then to see a mountain, and he was to climb the mountain. At the top of the mountain he would see a temple. She asked him to indicate when he saw the temple, and when he was there, they could begin their dialogue.

While she was guiding him, she saw the imagery herself. Sometimes this had happened to her in the past, but never with such exquisite detail. And while she was watching her own imagery, she continued to narrate to him, allowing him to create his own holy place. What she saw was a beautiful domed building. The outside entrances had white columns. The dome was golden. In the courtyard right outside the temple was a fountain with benches. Inside, she knew there was something very sacred, but only the very special ones were allowed entry.

"Jason, are you seeing the temple yet?"

"Oh yes. It's a white-columned circular building with a golden dome. I'm in a courtyard, around a fountain, and you are sitting on the bench, waiting for me."

Ali, who was seeing the exact same scenario, now found herself sitting beside him on the bench. "Jason, I recognize you now. We are connected on the soul level. That is why you were near my apartment the other day and you felt compelled to make a connection with me. Can you sense that, too?"

"Yeah, I feel that too. But it's so painful down there, I don't think it's worth it."

"Try to remember, Jason. We're all here for a reason. We all have something to do or something to learn."

"Jason sat for a while, with his head in his hands. Then I think they made a mistake with me. Why are you down there? Don't you find it hard, too?"

"Jason, I'd like you to look down from the mountain top and witness yourself sitting with me in my apartment?"

"Okay, I can do that."

"Tell me what you see."

"I see a wasted drug addict who is only sixteen and whose life is over. He is in constant pain because he sometimes remembers he's me, but he can't get here by himself. And sometimes he sees the hypocrisy and craziness of the world, and wonders if it can even survive, and he is ashamed to be a human being and part of the insanity. It doesn't make any sense to him to be there. But I know that he *does* has one more thing to do, and then he'll be done."

The Ali in the temple garden took his hand. All she felt was love for him. There was nothing to say. Her heart was so expanded. She told him how fortunate she felt for having met him on Earth as well as here. Then her guidance told her to finish the session. She told him to take three deep breaths and then she would count to ten and he would come back into this body. At the count of ten he opened his eyes and sat up.

He took a moment to reorient to the room and then bent over to put on his shoes. "Wow, that really felt true to me. So that's who I really am. That's beautiful . . . but I gotta go now."

Ali didn't feel ready to let him go. She wanted him to have something material to take home to remind him of his beautiful Self. She walked over to her bookshelf and picked out a small booklet of only about twenty pages. It contained fourteen poems by Kabir, translated by Robert Bly, and the title was the name of one of the poems: *The Fish in the Sea Is Not Thirsty.* She wrote her name and address on the inside cover and handed it to him.

"Jason, please take this. I think you'll find inspiration in this poetry, and maybe you'll see that the feelings you're having and the truths you've been experiencing are timeless, and that you're not alone."

He accepted the book and put it in his pocket. "Thanks again. I don't know how to thank you enough. I'm gonna try going back to the temple tonight in my dreams. Maybe you can meet me there. See ya."

Ali wondered why he felt he had to rush away, and noticed he hadn't finished his hot chocolate milk. She shook her head, and walked back into the kitchen to put the milk back in the refrigerator for tomorrow. She secretly hoped she could be a guide for him, and maybe the hot chocolate would be his version of her espresso.

Later that evening, when she wrote in her diary, Ali expressed the hopes that she would be his "Vio." She wanted so badly to do good in the world, and now here was an opportunity. During the past few weeks with Violetta she had, for the most part, only witnessed people in various life situations, but here was someone she could actually touch and influence. She wondered, as she put down those words, what Vio would have to say about it. There probably was a vestige—or more than a vestige—of ego in that goal, but why else was he sent to her this way? She expressed those sentiments when she wrote, "Why was he sent to me, if not for me to help him?" and she closed the evening's journaling session.

That night Ali had a dream. In the dream she went back to the field and saw the temple on the hill. She climbed the hill and found herself again sitting on a bench beside the fountain. She felt she was supposed to meet someone there and hoped it would be Jason. As soon as that thought entered her mind, a beautiful manifestation of Jason, with flowing white robes, walked over and sat beside her. He didn't seem so young anymore. He seemed very peaceful, like he was at a graduation ceremony and was very proud of his accomplishments. He again expressed his gratitude for her welcoming him into her home and admitted that he had been burglarizing her just two days earlier. She told him she had nothing to lose and valued him as a friend. He said he believed she wasn't telling the entire truth—that she *did* have something to lose. She thought for a while and then said, "I don't think so. I don't care about any material possessions anymore."

"Not a material possession. I know you don't care about those. But there is something you care about."

"Tell me."

"You'll see." And with that, he kissed her on the forehead, turned, and entered the temple.

18

No Show

The monk drew back the wooden mallet for a second time, and hit the bronze gong in its center. The sound reverberated in Ali's body as her eyes suddenly popped open, and she became aware that the source of the sound was her zen alarm clock on the table beside her bed.

Ali had set the alarm for nine, just in case Jason decided to come at ten—as he had the past two days. She didn't want him to catch her unprepared; so she jumped out of bed, showered and dressed, did a short meditation practice, ate a bagel, drank her coffee, and prepared the hot chocolate. She waited about thirty minutes and then reluctantly put Jason's drink back in the fridge. She had to admit, as stoic as she was, that she was very disappointed. She thought she'd helped him yesterday and was afraid that maybe he didn't value her enough. Who else could understand him the way she did? And she hadn't even shared with him the secret of Layla, the inter-dimensional dog.

Still holding the hope that he would come the following day, she went to the bedroom alcove, straightened out the bedclothes, and picked up her journal. The previous night's entry was again incorporated into the story, with another note. This time there was a star and then underlining under the phrase: "Why was he sent to me if not for me to help him?" At the bottom of the page she saw a star and the following question: "Have you ever considered that he was sent to help you?"

How was he helping me? She wondered. *We were always talking about him, weren't we? Oh yes, in the dream we talked about my not having attachments . . . . Oh.* She felt as if the breath had just been sucked out of her body. She lay back on the bed and stayed there for quite a while, totally deflated, physically, emotionally and spiritually, until she fell into a deep sleep.

19

Jason Leaves

Another day passed, and still Jason hadn't returned. At just about eleven a.m. she heard a voice coming from the speaker on the wall. "Miss Morgenstern, this is Detective Morrisey."

"Oh yes, Detective. As soon as I figure out this intercom I'll buzz you up."

Ali decided to open the door and await the detective in the hallway. As he approached, she saw he was carrying a book in his hand.

"Oh my God, that's my book! Where did you get that?" Her heart was beating, her breath stopped, anticipating his answer.

"This book was found on the body of a sixteen-year-old boy in Washington Square Park this morning. He OD'd on heroin during the night. The detective who was called to the scene brought the book into the station, and I was walking past his desk when I heard him mention that there was a name and address written inside the front cover. When he read off your name I recognized it, so I told him I knew the name from a burglary case I was working on, and that I'd return the book to you. This *is* your book, and I'm assuming it was removed from your apartment during the burglary. Is that correct?"

Ali took the book from his hand and shuffled through the pages. There was a rush of energy through her body, especially in her hands. Her fingers shook, and she almost dropped the book. She knew she needed to remain cool, so she regained her composure and said, "Yes, Officer. I didn't notice it was missing. I really appreciate your coming by with it. I guess you have your burglar now."

"Yes, this book *does* link him to your apartment and the incidents in your building."

Ali thanked him again for returning the book, and as soon as he was out the door, she held the book to her heart. *Oh Jason, Jason.* She lay down on her couch and allowed the energy to course through her body until her heartbeat returned to normal. She put the book on her meditation table, lit a candle and wrote his name on a small piece of paper. Then she watched the flame and reflected on the profound effect of her four-day relationship with Jason. She cried and cried, and she mourned him and his short life, and she wished she could have had more time with him; and she felt sadness for all the young ones who couldn't survive the denseness of this world.

And then she felt as if she'd been struck by lightning. She sat up and began to laugh and laugh and laugh. And as she laughed, all the tension left her body, and she felt so light she could almost fly. *Oh yes, yes. Vio was right. Jason, you were my teacher. I was trying so hard to save you, to heal you, to fix what I thought was broken, but all with my "small self." How can a "small self" fix anything when it doesn't even exist? It's all a misunderstanding. Jason, you shattered my ego's last argument for separation—that something is wrong, that something needs fixing, and that I, as the "small self" can do anything. And you showed me with my own book,* The Fish in the Sea Is Not Thirsty.

And Ali finally knew that she was—and always had been—swimming in a sea of love, and that she was the fish, and she was the sea, and there was no more thirst.

Twenty Years Later

Over the next twenty years, Ali lived alone in her loft with her inter-dimensional dog, Layla. She had achieved a simplicity she could never have imagined on the day she reluctantly took possession of Rose Cottage. Although she lived alone, she was rarely lonely, as many creative people gravitated around her. She held weekly gatherings of artists, dancers, writers, and musicians, which she called *Soirées*. During these evenings her guests would take turns performing for each other. Many felt they received inspiration from being in her presence—although she never took personal credit for this—not out of humility, but simply because she knew better.

Now that Ali was in her eighties, she found that she was most comfortable remaining in her loft; but the keys to the lake house were displayed on a hook by the door, and she made them available to any of her guests who asked. And thus the lake house continued to serve as a place of creativity and inspiration to many young artists over the years.

On a snowy evening in December, Ali was having a few friends and acquaintances over to the loft for one of her gatherings. As the performances came to a conclusion—with a cello and piano duet of Samuel Barber's *Adagio for Strings*—the light snow became a storm, and although most of the guests took their leave, one remained. He was a very distinguished tall, elderly gentleman with a full head of silver hair named Charles Hawkins. Since the storm didn't seem to be letting up, Ali suggested he spend the night and make his way home in the morning. Charles gratefully agreed to stay, and as Ali straightened up after the partygoers and prepared the roll-away bed, he glanced at some of the titles on her bookshelf. He became intrigued by a small book with a blue and purple cover and the strange title: *The Legacy of Violetta Rose.*

Charles removed the book from the shelf and approached Ali as she was putting away the last few dishes. "Ali, my dear, what is this book? I wonder why I've never heard of it before."

"Let me see what you have there." Ali lifted the book from his hand. "Oh, this is my journal. I haven't written in it for nearly twenty years. I don't know why, but I didn't seem to have a need to write anymore. Everything there was to say was said, I suppose. If you'd like, we could sit and read silently together for a while before we retire. I have my favorite poetry I like to read in the evenings."

"That would be marvelous," Charles replied. And he and Ali read well into the night. Ali became tired and excused herself, but Charles stayed up until morning, reading and re-reading this most fascinating account of a younger Ali and her guide Violetta Rose.

When morning came, Charles couldn't wait to tell Ali how enthralled he was with her book. As she served him a cup of tea, he made his request. "Ali, you know that I am a Broadway producer. I've been up all night reading this delightful book, and I would love your permission to produce your journal as a Broadway play."

"You have my permission, Charles, to do anything you'd like with it. But you know that it's incomplete."

"Yes, I noticed there were empty pages at the end. I'm sure we can come up with an appropriate ending. Would you like to be involved in the production process?"

"Oh no. I've done my part. I'll leave the rest to you. Let me know when it's produced and I will be happy to attend." It was clear she had no attachment to the writing or producing of this work, and having known her over the last twenty years, he was not surprised.

"May I take it with me today, have it copied, and get it back to you?"

"You may. It's now in your hands."

One Year Later

One year later, when the project was complete, Charles called Ali on the telephone to invite her to accompany him to the premiere. As he walked toward his desk to pick up the telephone, his eye was drawn to a small book on his shelf, with a blue and purple cover. He put down the phone and held the book in his hand once again. As he was leafing through it, he noticed that the book was no longer incomplete. He began to dial, and after three rings, he heard Ali's voice greeting him on the other end of the line.

"Good morning, this is Ali."

"Ali, darling, this is Charles. I am pleased to announce that the premiere of the play is on December tenth. I would be honored if you would attend as my special guest."

"Charles, I'd be delighted. December tenth, that is? That's a Friday then, isn't it?"

"Yes. I'll make a dinner reservation at Sardi's and I can pick you up in a limousine at five o'clock at your place, if that's acceptable to you. Showtime is at eight."

"That sounds excellent. I look forward to seeing you then. Is there anything else you wanted to ask me, Charles?"

"Oh yes, Ali. I find I've neglected to return the journal to you, and I apologize for that—"

"That's perfectly all right. I didn't miss it."

He continued, "Thank you for being so forgiving. Well, as I was saying, I was just looking through it, and I noticed that there were no longer empty pages at the end. Can you explain how that could have happened?"

"I'm not surprised, Charles. And if you have made yourself familiar with the journal, you shouldn't be surprised either."

"I suppose you're right. Would you like me to bring it over, and we can read the ending together?"

"Oh no," Ali responded immediately. "Let's live it instead. Don't you agree?"

He took a moment to process her response, and then realized that "living it" was the most appropriate thing to do. "Okay then. I'll see you on Friday night at five. The limo will be waiting." He hesitated for a moment, leafed through the last few pages, but averted his eyes from the words. *No, Ali is right*, and he closed the journal and placed it on his desk.

The evening went as planned. Charles arrived by limousine promptly at five and took her to an elegant pre-theater meal at Sardi's. They arrived at the theater in plenty of time.

They walked through the lobby, Ali, dressed in a long black velvet gown, with a white satin shawl—her silver hair loose, down to her waist—and Charles, handsome and distinguished, in his black tuxedo. She caught her reflection in the glass and was pleased to find that this time she was not invisible. He led her to their seats at the end of the first row, on the left aisle.

This time, Ali knew she was going to see the entire show. They watched a progression of characters, played beautifully by some very accomplished actors. In the first act there was, of course, the character Ali, at age sixty-one, receiving the prize of the house at Blue Swan Lake. Soon, the actress playing Violetta entered the stage. She looked remarkably as Ali remembered her, and the lighting was such that she truly looked translucent. They even had a real Wheaten Terrier who responded to the name "Layla." It all seemed so far away but also so familiar. Charles watched her reactions as each scene was played, and by her smiles and chuckles, he felt assured that his interpretation was to her liking. Act I ended with the theater scene, in which Ali was not permitted to see the show. She was grateful that Vio had presented it this way. Her life had been lived to the fullest, and no foreknowledge could have ever enhanced it in any way.

Act II began with the burglary and the policemen. She noticed that the actor who played the man with the rifle at the lake house in the second scene also played Detective Morrisey. "Charles," she whispered, "Does the same actor play the gunman and the policeman?"

"Oh yes. You noted a resemblance in your journal, and so we did our best to be true to your book."

"Of course," she recalled. "Well done."

Following the scene with the death of Jason, the play took on an entirely different tone—as did her life. There were no longer any lessons or visits from Violetta. Charles had decided to use this section of the play to showcase the talents of the people who actually had spent time at Ali's soirées over the years. He explained to her how every few months, they planned to change the content of the scene, so that different musicians, poets, dancers and writers would have a chance to show the New York theater audience their gifts. Ali approved heartily of this creative addition to the script. He then politely excused himself as he was to participate in the finale.

Ali watched, with pleasure, as the characters came out onto the stage to take their bows. Then the gunman/policeman jumped down from the stage and extended his hand to her. As the applause changed to shouts of "Author! Author!" she gently lifted the hem of her skirt and walked slowly and deliberately up the five steps to the stage. Charles, already waiting for her in the wings, took her left hand, and they walked to center stage as the audience stood up in their seats, applauding wildly. Ali turned to Charles and simply said, "You know I didn't write this." And then she bowed, and bowed and bowed . . . and the curtain fell for the last time.

APPENDIX

BOOKS FROM VIOLETTA'S LIBRARY

Barks, Coleman. *A Year with Rumi*. New York, NY: HarperCollins, 2006.

Barks, Coleman and John Moyne. *The Essential Rumi*. San Francisco: HarperCollins, 1995.

Bly, Robert. *The Kabir Book*. Boston, MA: Beacon Press, 1971.

Bly, Robert. *The Fish in the Sea Is Not Thirsty*. Northwood Narrows NH: Lillabulero Press, 1971.

Fox, Matthew. *Meditations with Meister Eckhart*. Santa Fe, NM: Bear & Company, 1983.

Haskel, Peter and Yoshita Hakeda, Editor. *Bankei Zen: Translations from the Record of Bankei*. New York, NY: Grove Press, 1984.

Kubose, the Venerable Gyomay, *Zen Koans*. Washington, DC: Henry Regenery Company, 1973.

Ladinsky, Daniel. *The Gift—Poems by Hafiz the Great Sufi Master*. New York, NY: Penguin, 1999.

Moyne, John and Coleman Barks. *Open Secret*. Putney, VT: Threshold Books, 1984.

Osborne, Arthur. *The Collected Works of Ramana Maharshi*, York Beach, ME: Samuel Weiser, Inc. , 1997.

Reps, Paul. *Zen Flesh, Zen Bones*. Garden City, NY: Anchor Books, n.d.

BOOKS ON WRITING

Bradbury, Ray. *Zen in the Art of Writing*. Santa Barbara, CA: Capra Press, 1990.

George, Elizabeth. *Write Away*. New York NY: HarperCollins, 2004.

Pressfield, Steven. *The War of Art: Break Through the Blocks and Win Your Inner Creative Battles*. New York NY: Warner Books Edition, 2002.

Sawyer, Robert J. *Relativity*. Dearfield, IL: ISFIC Press, 2004.

Stein, Sol. *Stein on Writing*. New York, NY: St. Martin's Press, 1995.

Wood, Monica. *The Pocket Muse: Ideas & Inspirations for Writing*. Cincinnati, OH: Writer's Digest Books, 2002.

_____. *The Pocket Muse: Endless Inspiration*. Cincinnati, OH: Writer's Digest Books, 2006.

Made in the USA